# ART *of*
# PRESERVING

# ART *of* PRESERVING

## JAN BERRY

PHOTOGRAPHY BY

## RODNEY WEIDLAND

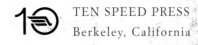

TEN SPEED PRESS
Berkeley, California

A Kirsty Melville Book

Ten Speed Press
P. O. Box 7123
Berkeley, California 94707

Distributed in Australia by E. J. Dwyer Pty. Ltd., in Canada by Publishers Group West,
in New Zealand by Tandem Press, in South Africa by Real Books, in the United Kingdom
and Europe by Airlift Books, and in Singapore and Malaysia by Berkeley Books.

Produced in association with
Barbara Beckett Publishing
14 Hargrave Street, Paddington, Sydney, Australia 2021

Design by Barbara Beckett and Megan Smith
Edited by Julia Cain

Library of Congress Cataloging-in-Publication Data

Berry, Jan.
Art of preserving/Jan Berry: photography by Rodney Weidland.
ISBN 0-898 15-895-8 (paper)
1. Canning and preserving. I. Title.
TX603. B435 1997
641. 4--dc21

96-29491
CIP

First printing, 1997
Printed in Hong Kong

2 3 4 5 6 - 99 98 97

ACKNOWLEDGMENTS
Sincere thanks to Barbara Beckett for her
expertise and cheerfulness in making this book
happen. To Julia Cain who so ably and efficiently
edited the manuscript, Kirsty Melville of Ten
Speed Press for her confidence in us, and to
Rodney who makes working together so
pleasurable.
J. B.

# CONTENTS

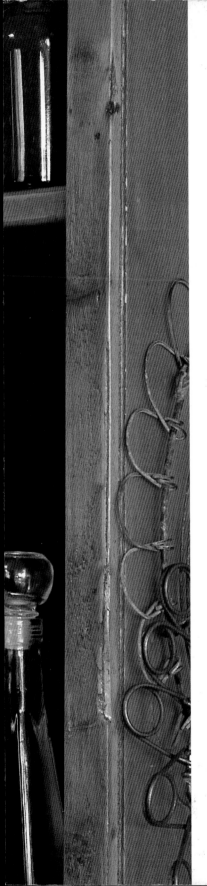

# THE *Basics*
## OF *Preserving*

*The nectarine, and curious peach,*

*Into my hands themselves do reach;*

*Stumbling on melons, as I pass,*

*Ensnared with flowers, I fall on grass.*

ANDREW MARVELL

*LEFT: I like to decorate the jars of preserves after they have been bottled, creating more pleasure, not just for myself, but for my family and friends.*

Good food begins with good shopping. Whatever food item you are buying, there is no substitute for quality, so be a canny shopper. Buy seasonally, keeping an eye open for bargains, and remember to buy good quality ingredients in the right condition for your recipe. All ingredients should be as fresh as possible and free from blemishes. You'll want just under-ripe oranges for jams and marmalades but fully ripe tomatoes for tomato sauce. Fruit is better a little under-ripe for making jam as it sets better than overripe fruit.

Wash all fruit and vegetables and dry them with paper towels. Fruit and vegetables to be used with the skin on should be scrubbed.

## JARS

Jars are available in various sizes and styles from cookware shops and supermarkets. It is fine to reuse jars, provided the lids and the tops of the jars are not damaged in any way. Check the amount the recipe makes and check your jars by filling and measuring them with water. This will help you sterilize the correct number of jars. If the jars do not have tight-fitting lids, replace the lids with cellophane jar covers.

## STERILIZATION

Jars and lids should be sterilized before use. An easy way to do this is to place the clean jars and lids in the dishwasher and run them through a hot rinse cycle. Jars can also be washed carefully and then sterilized in the oven. Place them upright on a baking tray in a cold oven, turn the heat to 250°F (120°C), and leave for 30 minutes. Remove the jars from the oven and cover them with a clean dishcloth until ready to use. This is a simpler method, and far less dangerous, than boiling jars and lids in water for 20 minutes.

## WARMING JARS

Always pot jams, jellies, and chutneys into warmed, sterilized, dry jars. Place the jars on a wooden board and be very careful — hot jam is hot sugar and can cause nasty burns. Use a ladle, cup, or small jug to transfer the jam to the jars, and, if available, a wide-mouthed jam funnel. Wipe the jars clean while they are still hot with a hot, damp dishcloth and make sure there are no air bubbles — disperse these by running a skewer down the inside of the jar.

## SEALING JARS

Generally cover the jars while hot, unless stated otherwise in the recipe. Place a round of waxed or parchment paper on top, followed by a tight-fitting lid. Cellophane jar covers can be used and are available from supermarkets and kitchen shops. Check that the lids are screwed on tight or tied down. Always label each jar with the name and date.

## STORAGE

Store all preserves in a cool, dry place away from direct sunlight.

## SHELF LIFE

All the recipes included in this book have been chosen for their flavor and keeping qualities but it must be remembered that they do not contain any preservatives and therefore care must be taken with storage and shelf life. All preserves should be refrigerated once a jar is opened.

QUANTITIES

It is difficult to tell the exact quantity each recipe will make as this will vary with the ripeness and juiciness of the fruit, the thickness you prefer for your chutney or jam, and the amount of liquid the seeds absorb during cooking. Even the shape of the jam pan or saucepan can make a difference. A wider pan will cause more rapid evaporation, the fruit will not need to cook for so long, and will taste fresher. I have estimated quantities in cups where 1 cup is equal to a container that holds 8 fluid ounces or 250 mL.

## Jams and marmalades

A well-made jam is a joy to behold. It should be transparent and the color of the original fruit. All jams and marmalades will keep for 6 to 12 months. Store them in a cool, dry place. Awareness of the following factors will ensure you success:

SUGAR

Sugar is the most important ingredient in making jam. Always use the best quality sugar stated in the recipe. Use white granulated sugar unless otherwise specified.

It is important to heat the sugar before adding it to the hot fruit and liquid. This is to avoid lowering the temperature already reached. Warm the sugar in a baking dish, about 1 inch (3 cm) deep, in a cool oven at 250°F (120°C) for 10 minutes. Do not overheat the sugar. Add the sugar to the hot fruit and stir until the sugar dissolves, then bring the mixture to a boil. If the fruit is not cooked before you add the sugar, it will harden and the jam will be cloudy.

PECTIN AND ACID

A good set in the jam is gained when the fruit selected has the right amount of pectin and acid in it, or when a fruit with high pectin and acid is added. Jams require acid to act with the pectin in the fruit to make them set. The fruit should be fresh and slightly under-ripe, as that is when it has the most pectin. The fruit needs to be cooked gently for some time in order to break down the cell walls and extract the acid.

Some fruits such as strawberries, cherries, and pears lack acid and require the addition of an acid in the form of lemon juice, tartaric acid, or citric acid (crystallized sour salt). The acid improves the color of the jam.

Pectin is a substance found to some extent in all fruits. Some fruits are higher in pectin than others and ensure a good setting jam. The fruits with the highest amount of pectin include apples, plums, lemons, quinces, and red currants. Fruits low in pectin, such as pears, strawberries, and mulberries, may require the addition of commercial pectin or lemon juice to make a good set.

Pectin is found in the seeds and pith of citrus fruits, so, when slicing the fruit, remove the seeds and tie them in a muslin bag. Remove the bag when the fruit is cooked, just before you add the sugar. When making marmalade, squeeze the bag over the pan as hard as possible to let the pectin drop back in.

Marmalade, a mixture of jelly and fruit, takes longer to cook than jam — it may take up to 2 hours before the sugar is added. To prevent all the fruit from rising to the top of the jar, allow the marmalade to cool slightly, about 10 to 15 minutes, before bottling. The marmalade will then thicken a little and, if it is stirred carefully before it is ladled into the jars, the fruit will disperse through the jelly. This also applies to berry jam, especially strawberry.

## SKIMMING JAM

Skim the top of the jam only if necessary, skimming the scum and not the foam. If you are using good quality sugar this shouldn't be necessary.

## SETTING POINT

To test if a jam is set, place a teaspoonful onto a very cold plate taken straight from the freezer. Push the jam with your finger. If it wrinkles and is reasonably stiff, the jam is set. This setting point, which occurs at 220°F (105°C), can also be tested with a warmed thermometer.

## JAM-MAKING EQUIPMENT

Good jam-making equipment is a really worthwhile investment if you are serious about making jam. Successful jam making begins with a suitable pan. It should have a wide top and slightly sloping sides to allow the water to evaporate quickly without overcooking the fruit. 'Jelling' is then achieved faster, which is preferable to a longer cooking time. Preserving or jam pans can be made of aluminum and some are nonstick. Copper pans are traditional, but very expensive. They look beautiful and conduct the heat well. Side handles, or an upright handle which stays cool, are ideal.

Long-handled wooden spoons are best for stirring. A skimmer with a long handle is good for removing scum or lifting out stones, pits, and seeds from the fruit as they rise to the top.

I don't use a thermometer, but some cooks feel happier to check that the jam is ready, at about 220°F (105°C). If you are a little unsure and new to jam making, a thermometer will avoid the problem of overcooking. Jam can overcook very quickly, causing it to darken and harden.

Jam funnels, which are available from cookware shops, are inexpensive and well worth buying. They help avoid spilling and reduce the possibility of nasty burns. Funnels have a broad top and a large neck, and will fit large and small jars.

## Jellies

Fruit need not be peeled or cored when making jelly. Just wash and roughly chop large fruit. There is no need to husk or hull berries.

The usual proportion for cooking fruit is about 4 cups (1 liter) of water to each pound (500 g) of fruit. Cook the fruit until it is tender, then strain it through a jelly bag.

*Right: A basket full of jars of preserves ready to take to the local school fête.*

Jelly bags are very reasonably priced, and it is preferable to use one. If a jelly bag is not available, tie a clean linen dishcloth to all four legs of an upside-down stool or chair that has been safely anchored on a table or bench. Place a bowl underneath the bag or cloth. Pour boiling water through the jelly bag or dishcloth just prior to using it. This ensures absolute cleanliness and wets and heats the fabric to allow the fruit juices to drip through more freely. Never squeeze the jelly bag or try to force the juice through the bag, as this will cloud the jelly.

Add sugar to the juice in the proportion of 1 pound (500 g) sugar to 2 cups (500 mL) of strained juice. Then boil the jelly until it reaches setting point, as for jam. A good set on a jelly is a little wobbly.

Sterilize the jars, warm them for bottling, and cover them while hot. When bottling, be careful not to move the jars until the jelly is well set. I leave them overnight before storing them. Use small jars to help get a good set.

Jellies are best stored in a cool, dry, dark place because the color and flavor can deteriorate if exposed to light. All jellies will keep for 6 to 12 months.

## Chutneys, relishes, and sauces

These simple preparations make good use of an abundance of produce in season. They improve with keeping and are best kept for a minimum of 1 month before eating.

BELOW: *A fall harvest of mushrooms waiting to be preserved for the coming month: chanterelles, cêpes, and field mushrooms.*

Fruit and vegetables for chutneys, relishes, and sauces need not be of the highest quality, but they should be ripe. A few blemishes won't matter, as they can be cut out. Using a good quality vinegar is essential. When not using malt or cider vinegars, use a fermented wine vinegar. White or brown sugar can be used. In general, the darker colors will produce darker looking chutneys and the longer you cook the chutney, the darker it will be.

A nonreactive saucepan with a heavy base is ideal for chutney making. Copper and brass react with vinegar and salt, so an enamel or stainless steel saucepan is recommended instead.

Generally all ingredients are placed in the saucepan, with the whole spices tied in a muslin bag to be removed when the chutney is cooked. Some recipes require the vegetables or fruit to be cooked a little before the sugar is added. Chutney takes between 1 to 2 hours to cook and needs to be stirred towards the end as the fruit may start sticking to the pan.

The saucepan is not usually covered during cooking and the chutney is done when the fruit or vegetables are tender and the chutney thickens. To test if the chutney is ready, draw a wooden spoon along the bottom of the saucepan. If there is no free liquid emerging, the chutney is the correct thickness. This is known as setting point.

Bottle chutney in sterilized jars, the same way as for jam. Let it cool a little before ladling it into the jars. Make sure there are no air bubbles when bottling — remove them by running a skewer down the inside of each jar. Cover the chutney jars after they have cooled. Do not use metal lids unless they are plastic lined. Chutneys like to be stored in the dark and will keep for 6 to 8 months.

## Pickles

Homemade pickles have a special quality that elevates them above their commercial counterpart in flavor and texture. The great variety that can be made at home are usually very much cheaper, not to mention satisfying, to make. When you feel you have mastered pickle-making, experiment with different herb and spice combinations and a range of vinegars.

Ingredients should be of the highest quality and not overripe. Cider and wine vinegars have the best flavor for pickles, and white wine vinegar, being clear, gives a more attractive pickle. Use sea salt rather than table salt because it is natural and has no additives. Vinegar should always be brought to a boil before proceeding with a recipe.

Sterilize jars as for jams. When bottling, take care that the vinegar completely covers the contents of the jar (this may need to be topped up during storage). Do not use metal lids unless they are plastic lined. Make sure there are no air bubbles — remove them by running a skewer down the inside of each jar.

Pickles do not keep quite as well as chutney, so they are best made in smaller batches and eaten sooner. Pickles will keep for up to 6 months, stored in a cool, dark place.

# Citrus Fruits

The oranges of the Island are like blazing fire

Amongst the emerald boughs

And the lemons are like the paleness of a lover

Who has spent the night crying . . ...

MOHAMMED IBN OMAR

*LEFT: Lemons, limes, tangelos, oranges, and grapefruits are among the most colorful of the citrus fruits.*

# BLOOD ORANGE MARMALADE

*If blood oranges are not available, substitute oranges or tangelos. Do not peel the fruit!*

### INGREDIENTS
*8 firm blood oranges*
*2 lemons*
*6 cups (1.5 liters) water*
*5 cups (2½ pounds/1.25 kg)*
  *white granulated sugar,*
  *warmed*
*½ cup (125 mL) whiskey*

Thinly slice the oranges and lemons, catching any juice. Place the fruit slices and juice in a bowl, cover with the water, and leave for 12 hours. Transfer the fruit and water to a jam pan or a large, wide saucepan, and bring to a boil over medium heat. Reduce the heat and simmer until the rind is soft, about 40 minutes. Add the warmed sugar, stirring until the sugar dissolves. Increase the heat and boil until setting point is reached, about 30 minutes. Stir in the whiskey. Leave to settle for 10 minutes, then spoon the marmalade into warmed, sterilized jars and seal when cool.

MAKES ABOUT 4 CUPS

# ORANGE CHUTNEY

*Refreshing citrus flavors complement foods from biscuits to roasts.*

### INGREDIENTS
*5 large, firm oranges*
*3 large onions, sliced*
*2 tablespoons sea salt*
*3 large cooking apples*
*1 cup (5 ounces/155 g) dates*
*2 cups (500 mL) cider vinegar*
*2 cups (10 ounces/310 g)*
  *brown sugar*
*1 teaspoon ground ginger*
*1 tablespoon mustard seeds*
*½ teaspoon each chile (chilli)*
  *powder and ground cloves*

Chop the oranges, with peels on, into small cubes and discard any seeds. Place the oranges and onions in a large bowl, sprinkle with the salt, and leave to stand overnight, covered.

The next day, strain off the liquid. Peel and chop the apples and chop the pitted dates. Place the oranges and onions in a nonreactive pan and add all the remaining ingredients. Bring the mixture to a boil over medium heat, stirring occasionally. Cook until the orange skin is tender and the chutney has thickened, about 45 to 60 minutes. Ladle the chutney into warmed, sterilized jars and seal.

MAKES ABOUT 6 TO 8 CUPS

# SPICED ORANGE SLICES

*Oranges are usually eaten fresh, juiced, or in salads, but they also preserve very well.*

INGREDIENTS
*10 large, firm oranges*
*2⅓ cups (600 mL) white wine*
  *vinegar*
*4 cups (2 pounds/1 kg) white*
  *granulated sugar*
*1 cinnamon stick*
*6 cloves*
*4 blades of mace*

Cut the oranges, with peels on, into ¼ inch (6 mm) slices. Place the slices in a preserving pan or a large, wide saucepan and just cover with water. Bring the water to a boil and simmer, covered, until the slices are soft, about 45 minutes. Set aside. In another saucepan, combine the vinegar, sugar, cinnamon stick, cloves, and mace, bring to a boil, and cook for 5 minutes. Set aside. Strain the oranges slices, reserving the liquid. In batches of about 10 slices each, place the orange slices in the vinegar syrup, bring to a boil, and cook over medium heat for 30 minutes. If the syrup reduces, add some of the reserved liquid. When all the slices are cooked and placed in a dish, pour over any syrup, cover, and leave to marinate for 12 hours. Return the slices and syrup to the pan and reboil to thicken the syrup. Spoon into warmed, sterilized, wide-necked jars and seal.

MAKES ABOUT 4 CUPS

# ORANGE RATAFIA

*Bitter oranges, such as the Seville, are mostly used in marmalade and liqueurs.*

INGREDIENTS
*6 firm oranges*
*4 cups (1 liter) brandy*
*1 cup (8 ounces/250 g) white*
  *granulated sugar*
*½ cup cloves*
*½ cup allspice berriess*

Remove the orange peel with a vegetable peeler, leaving behind the white pith, which is very bitter. Slice the peel finely. Squeeze the juice from the oranges and place the juice and the peel in a large jar. Add the brandy, sugar, cloves, and allspice berries and stir well. Seal and place the jar in a cool, dark, dry place for 2 to 3 months. Strain the liqueur, pour it into a sterilized bottle, and seal well. Store the ratafia in a cool place. The liqueur is ready to drink immediately.

MAKES ABOUT 3 CUPS

# BLOOD ORANGE POMANDER BRANDY

*Serve this aromatic orange liqueur with coffee or dessert. It looks so beautiful that a bottle makes a perfect gift. If blood oranges are not in season, use any type of orange.*

INGREDIENTS
*1 large, firm blood orange*
*20 cloves*
*½ cup (4 ounces/125 g) brown sugar*
*½ cinnamon stick*
*2 cups (500 mL) brandy*

Using a paring knife, remove a continuous piece of peel from around the orange. Discard the peel. Push the cloves into the peel left on the orange. Place the orange in a wide-necked, sterilized jar, add the sugar and cinnamon stick, and cover with brandy. Seal the jar and store it in a cool, dark place for a minimum of 3 months. Strain the brandy from the jar into a sterilized bottle and seal well.

MAKES ABOUT 2 CUPS

# ORANGE WINE

*Use a dry white wine (but not necessarily an expensive one) for this recipe. Serve Orange Wine as a dessert wine or as a long drink with ice and mineral water. For a more complex flavor, try garnishing it with a flavored sage, such as pineapple sage.*

INGREDIENTS
*2 large, ripe oranges*
*1⅔ cups (13 ounces/405 g) granulated cube sugar*
*4 cups (1 liter) riesling or other dry white wine*

*RIGHT: I make Blood Orange Pomander Brandy when blood oranges are in season. I can't resist the beauty of the blood-red tint that spreads like a blush across the orange flesh.*

Remove the orange peel with a vegetable peeler, leaving the pith on. Slice the peel into strips. Place the strips in a 4-cup (1-liter) jar and add the sugar and the wine. Seal and leave the jar in a sunny place for 2 to 3 weeks.

Shake the jar daily. Strain the wine and decant it into sterilized bottles. Seal the bottles well and store them in a cool, dark place for up to 12 months. The wine is ready to use after 1 month.

MAKES ABOUT 4 CUPS

# CHUNKY GRAPEFRUIT

*Serve Chunky Grapefruit Marmalade on slices of thick toast at breakfast.*

INGREDIENTS

*3 large, firm grapefruits, cubed, seeds and juice reserved*

*3 large, firm lemons, sliced thinly, seeds and juice reserved*

*6 cups (1.5 liters) water*

*About 6 cups (3 pounds/ 1.5 kg) white granulated sugar*

Place all the fruit and juice into a bowl and cover it with the water. Put the seeds in a muslin bag and add it to the bowl. Allow to stand, covered, overnight. Transfer to a jam pan or a large, wide saucepan over medium heat and cook until the grapefruit skin is soft and half the liquid has evaporated, about 1 hour. Remove and discard the muslin bag. Measure the pulp and return it to the pan, adding 1 cup (8 ounces/ 250 g) sugar for each cup of pulp. Bring to a boil over medium heat, stirring until the sugar dissolves. Turn the heat to high and boil rapidly until setting point is reached, about 30 minutes. Remove the pan from the heat and stir for 3 to 5 minutes to distribute the fruit. Ladle the marmalade into warmed, sterilized jars and seal.

MAKES ABOUT 8 CUPS

# CITRUS MARMALADE

*In this refreshing marmalade, a touch of brandy rounds out the sharp citrus taste.*

INGREDIENTS

*4 pounds (2 kg) firm oranges, chopped*

*3 firm lemons, chopped*

*3 cups (1 pound/500 g) raisins*

*12 cups (3 liters) cold water*

*12 cups (6 pounds/3 kg) white granulated sugar, warmed*

*1 tablespoon corn syrup (golden syrup)*

*⅓ cup (90 mL) brandy*

Place oranges, lemons, raisins, and water in a jam pan or a large, wide saucepan over medium heat. Bring the water to a boil and cook until the fruit peel is tender and the liquid is reduced by half, about 1 hour. Add the warmed sugar and corn syrup and stir until the sugar dissolves. Bring the mixture to a boil, and boil rapidly until setting point is reached, about 30 minutes. Stir in the brandy, remove the pan from the heat, and continue to stir for 3 minutes to distribute the fruit. Leave to stand for 5 minutes, stir again, then ladle into warmed, sterilized jars. Seal the jars when cool.

MAKES ABOUT 10 CUPS

# GRAPEFRUIT JAM

*Some grapefruits have very thick skins with a lot of pith. It is best to use fruit without much pith because the pith makes the jam bitter.*

INGREDIENTS

*2 pounds (1 kg) ripe grapefruit*

*3 firm lemons*

*8 cups (2 liters) water*

*4 tablespoons preserved ginger, finely chopped*

*6 cups (3 pounds/1.5 kg) white granulated sugar, warmed*

Peel the grapefruits and the lemons with a vegetable peeler, leaving the pith on the fruit. Finely slice the peel and place it in a jam pan or a large, wide saucepan. Cut the pith from the fruit and reserve. Cut the fruit into small pieces, reserving the seeds, and add the fruit to the jam pan. Tie the pith and the seeds in a muslin bag and place the bag in the jam pan. Pour in the water. Bring the mixture to a boil and then simmer until the peel is tender and the liquid is reduced by about one-third, about 10 to 15 minutes. Add the ginger and the warmed sugar, stirring, until the sugar dissolves. Bring back to a boil and boil rapidly until setting point is reached, about 30 minutes. Remove the pan from the heat and allow it to stand for 10 minutes. Stir the jam well and then ladle it into warmed, sterilized jars and seal.

MAKES ABOUT 4 CUPS

*RIGHT: This is my favorite recipe for Grapefruit Jam. The jam is flavored with ginger and has a very fine texture.*

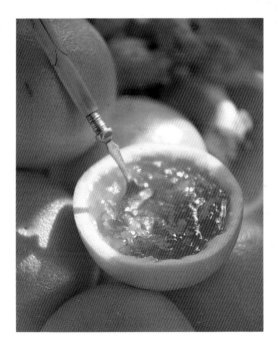

# LIME MARMALADE

*Enjoy the lovely pale green tones of this marmalade as well as the refreshing qualities of the limes.*

INGREDIENTS
*12 ripe limes*
*12 cups (3 liters) cold water*
*White granulated sugar*

Peel the zest from the limes with a vegetable peeler and cut it into very fine shreds. Cut the white pith from the limes and reserve. Chop the flesh into fine slices and reserve any seeds. Place the lime slices and any juice, along with the zest shreds, into a jam pan or a large, wide saucepan. Tie the pith and the seeds into a muslin bag and add it to the pan. Add the water and place the pan over medium heat. Bring to a boil and simmer until the liquid is reduced by half. Squeeze and discard the muslin bag. Measure the pulp and return it to the pan, adding 1 cup (8 ounces/250 g) sugar for each cup of pulp. Bring the mixture to a boil over medium heat and boil the marmalade rapidly until setting point is reached, about 30 minutes. Skim off any scum on the surface. Remove the pan from the heat and let it stand for 10 minutes. Stir well and then ladle the marmalade into warmed, sterilized jars and seal them when the marmalade is cool.
MAKES ABOUT 8 CUPS

*LEFT: I make quantities of Lime Marmalade when limes are in season and inexpensive.*

---

LIMES

Limes are native to northeastern India and southeast Asia but they are now grown throughout the tropics and subtropics where there is no chance of frost. The flavor is more intense than that of the lemon, so when substituting for lemon, use a lesser quantity of lime. Look for a firm, shiny, green skin and avoid limes with pale, wrinkled skins.

Lime juice is excellent to use for squeezing over foods to bring out their flavor, or as an additive to alcoholic and non-alcoholic drinks. Lime juice or Lemonade made with lime (page 27) make the most of lime's refreshing qualities, unequalled by most other fruits.

# LEMON OIL

*Lemon oil is very simple to make. It is very attractive to look at and is great for salad dressing or for brushing onto chicken or fish before roasting or grilling.*

INGREDIENTS
*4 firm lemons*
*A few lemon leaves, washed*
  *and dried*
*A few peppercorns*
*Extra virgin olive oil*

Cut the the lemons into quarters and remove any obvious seeds. Pack the lemon quarters into a wide-necked, sterilized jar. Place a couple of lemon leaves and a few peppercorns in the jar. Pour in enough olive oil to cover the lemons and then seal the jar. Allow the lemons to steep for at least 6 weeks before using the oil. The oil may be strained off to use from the jar, and the lemons are discarded when the oil is finished. Store the oil in a cool, dark place.
MAKES 1 4-CUP JAR

# LEMON CURD

*Lemons originated in India but are now grown worldwide in warm, temperate climates. The lemon is versatile in its culinary uses and is never absent from my kitchen.*

INGREDIENTS
*4 large, firm lemons*
*½ cup (4 ounces/125 g ) butter*
*1½ cups (12 ounces/375 g)*
  *white granulated sugar*
*4 large eggs, beaten*

Zest the lemon rind (the curd must be free of pith). Squeeze the lemons and strain the juice. In a double boiler, melt the butter, add the lemon zest and juice, sugar, and beaten eggs. Cook the mixture over low heat for 20 to 30 minutes, whisking from time to time. The mixture should be smooth and creamy. Ladle the curd into warmed, sterilized jars and seal at once. Store the curd in a cool, dark place.
MAKES ABOUT 2 CUPS

*RIGHT: The first stage in making Lemon Oil (this page), Lemon Curd (this page), and Preserved Lemons (page 26).*

# PRESERVED LEMONS

*To use the preserved lemons, rinse them, cut them into strips or dice the peel and flesh, and add them to chicken, lamb, or fish dishes. And don't throw away the juice from the preserved lemons—use it to make a vinaigrette or marinade.*

INGREDIENTS
8 to 10 thin-skinned lemons
½ cup sea salt
2 cinnamon sticks
2 bay leaves
8 peppercorns
2 cardamom pods
Juice of 2 lemons
Olive oil

Scrub the lemons thoroughly to remove any scales. Place them in a bowl of cold water and leave for 3 days at room temperature, changing the water daily. Next, cut each lemon into quarters from the top to about ⅜ inch (1 cm) from the bottom so that the lemon remains intact. Sprinkle the inside of each lemon with the sea salt. Place the lemons in a large, sterilized jar. Sprinkle over any remaining salt, and add the cinnamon sticks, bay leaves, peppercorns, and cardamom pods. Add the lemon juice and top up the jar with olive oil. Store the lemons in a very cool, dry place for up to 6 months. Leave for 1 month before using.
MAKES 1 8-CUP JAR

# LEMON VINEGAR

*Use this aromatic vinegar in dressings and vinaigrettes. Use a vegetable peeler or a paring knife to make the twirls of lemon zest.*

INGREDIENTS
4 cups (1 liter) white wine
    vinegar
2 cups (500 mL) white wine
Zest of 4 lemons, cut into
    twirls
6 cloves garlic, peeled and
    lightly crushed
1 bunch lemon-scented thyme
3 bay leaves
1 extra lemon

Place all the ingredients except the extra lemon in a large, sterilized, screw-top jar or a covered crock, seal, and allow the mixture to infuse at room temperature for at least 1 month.

Strain the lemon vinegar and decant it into sterilized bottles. Discard the contents of the sieve. Make some extra twirls of lemon zest and add them to each bottle. Store the vinegar in a cool, dark place.
MAKES ABOUT 6 CUPS

# LEMONADE

*This refreshing drink is also splendid made from lime juice.*

INGREDIENTS

*8 large, firm lemons or 10
limes*

*4 cups (2 pounds/1 kg ) white
granulated sugar*

*¾ ounce (25 g) citric acid
(crystallised sour salt)*

*6 cups (1.5 liters) boiling water*

Remove the lemon rind with a vegetable peeler. Cut the rind into very thin strips. Squeeze the juice from the lemons and add it to the sugar in a bowl, along with the lemon rind strips and the citric acid. Add the boiling water and stir well until the sugar dissolves. Leave to cool, then strain into screw-top or resealable sterilized bottles. The lemonade is best stored in the refrigerator.

MAKES ABOUT 6 CUPS

# MANDARIN JELLY

*The red-orange varieties of mandarin make an especially attractive, colorful jelly.*

INGREDIENTS

*3 pounds (1.5 kg) firm
mandarins, cubed, seeds and
juice reserved*

*2 firm lemons, cubed, seeds
and juice reserved*

*½ ounce (15 g) citric acid
(crystallized sour salt)*

*11 cups (2.75 liters) water*

*7 cups (3½ pounds/1.75 kg)
white granulated sugar*

Place the fruit, reserved juice, and seeds tied up in a muslin bag in a large bowl, add the citric acid and water, and let stand, covered, for 12 hours or overnight.

Transfer the contents of the bowl to a jam pan or a large, wide saucepan over medium heat. Bring to a boil, lower the heat, and simmer for 1 to 1½ hours or until the rind is soft. Remove and discard the muslin bag. Pour the mixture into a jelly bag and leave it to drip overnight or for 12 hours. Discard the fruit pulp left in the bag.

Pour the strained liquid into the cleaned pan and add the sugar. Place the pan over medium heat and stir until the sugar dissolves. Bring the mixture to a boil over high heat and boil rapidly until setting point is reached, about 30 minutes. Ladle the jelly into warmed, sterilized jars and seal when cold. The jelly is ready to use after 2 weeks.

MAKES ABOUT 4 CUPS

# KUMQUAT JAM

*This jam, made from the "little gem" of the citrus family, is ready to use after 3 weeks.*

### INGREDIENTS

*2 pounds (1 kg) firm kumquats, sliced, seeds reserved and tied up in a muslin bag*
*6 cups (1.5 liters) water*
*8 cups (4 pounds/2 kg) white granulated sugar, warmed*
*Juice of 3 lemons*

Place the fruit in a bowl and add the muslin bag. Add the water, cover, and leave overnight. The next day, place the contents of the bowl in a jam pan or a large, wide saucepan and squeeze in the gluey pectin from the muslin bag. Place the pan over medium heat and bring to a slow boil. Cook until the fruit is tender and the liquid is reduced by half, about 40 minutes. Add the warmed sugar and stir until it dissolves. Add the lemon juice. Continue to boil until setting point is reached, about 30 minutes. Ladle the jam into warmed, sterilized jars. Cover and seal.

MAKES ABOUT 4 CUPS

# TROPICAL MARMALADE

*This unusual blend of flavors yields a marmalade like no other.*

### INGREDIENTS

*4 ripe tangerines or mandarins, peel reserved and shredded*
*2 ripe lemons, peel reserved and shredded*
*1 small, ripe pineapple*
*10 cups (2.5 liters) water*
*10 cups (5 pounds/2.5 kg) white sugar, warmed*
*5 fluid ounces (155 mL) sherry*

*RIGHT: I enjoy the texture and acidic sweetness of Kumquat Jam.*

Remove the pith from the lemons and reserve. Cut the tangerine and lemon flesh into small pieces, reserving the seeds. Place the flesh in a jam pan or a large, wide saucepan. Peel and core the pineapple (reserve the trimmings). Chop the flesh and peel and add it to the pan. Place the lemon pith and seeds and the pineapple peel and core into muslin, tie it up into a bag, and add it to the pan. Pour in the water. Place the pan over medium heat, bring to a boil, and simmer until the water is reduced by half, about 20 minutes. Add the warmed sugar and stir until the sugar dissolves. Increase the heat and boil rapidly until setting point is reached, about 30 minutes. Add the sherry and continue to boil for 5 minutes. Remove the pan from the heat and discard the muslin bag, squeezing the pectin into the jam. Stand for 5 minutes, stir well, then ladle into warmed, sterilized jars and seal.

MAKES ABOUT 4 CUPS

# CANDIED CITRUS PEEL

*Any citrus peel can be used to make candied fruit. Serve the peel with espresso coffee.*

INGREDIENTS

*2 large citrus fruits, such as*
  *lemon, mandarin, tangerine,*
  *tangelo, pink grapefruit, or*
  *any other variety*
*Water*
*2 cups (1 pound/500 g) white*
  *granulated sugar*
*Extra 1 cup (8 ounces/250g)*
  *white granulated sugar*

Cut a thin slice of peel from the top and the bottom of each piece of fruit. Cut vertical strips from the top to the bottom about ¾ inch (2 cm) apart, cutting through the skin and the pith of the fruit. Remove the strips of peel and cut them into thinner strips, about ⅜ inch (1 cm) wide. Place the peel in a saucepan and cover it with 8 cups (2 liters) water. Bring the water to a boil over high heat and cook until the peel is soft when tested with a skewer, about 15 minutes. Drain and reserve the peel. Place 2 cups (500 mL) water in a saucepan and add the sugar. Bring the water to a boil, stirring until the sugar dissolves. Remove the saucepan from the heat and stir in the peel. Leave to stand for 8 hours at room temperature.

Place the saucepan over low heat until the peel has absorbed all of the syrup, about 30 minutes. Watch it carefully towards the end of the cooking time or the peel can burn. Remove the peel from the pan with tongs and spread it out on aluminum foil. Leave to stand for 12 hours.

The next day, coat the peel one piece at a time in the extra sugar. Dry it on a cake rack for 3 hours. Pack the candied peel into airtight tins or jars layered with waxed paper. Store the peel in a cool, dry place for up to 2 months.
MAKES ABOUT 1 4-CUP JAR

*LEFT: The fragile beauty of*
*Candied Citrus Peel. This peel*
*has been made from citron, but*
*lime or grapefruit peel will give a*
*similar effect.*

MANDARINS, TANGERINES, AND TANGELOS
The mandarin is probably a hybrid of the sweet orange, and is most likely native to southern China. Some types of red-orange mandarin, known as tangerines, acquired their name when they travelled to Europe via the city of Tangiers in North Africa. A tangelo is a cross between a tangerine and a pomelo, a sweet thick-skinned precursor to grapefruit.

# WHISKEY TANGELO MARMALADE

*Tangelos are a delicious fruit eaten fresh and in salads. They also make lovely marmalade.*

INGREDIENTS
*5 firm tangelos, peeled, thinly sliced, juice and seeds reserved*
*3 firm lemons, peeled, thinly sliced, juice and seeds reserved*
*4 cups (1 liter) boiling water*
*4 cups (2 pounds/1 kg) white granulated sugar, warmed*
*¼ cup (60 mL) whiskey*

Place the fruit slices and juice in a bowl. Put the seeds into a muslin bag and add it to the bowl. Pour over the boiling water and leave for 1 hour. Place the fruit and water in a jam pan or a large, wide saucepan; squeeze the contents of the muslin bag into the pan and then discard the bag. Bring the mixture to a boil and simmer over medium heat for 1 hour. Add the warmed sugar, stirring until the sugar dissolves. Bring the mixture to a boil and cook until setting point is reached and the mixture is clear, about 30 to 40 minutes, then stir in the whiskey. Skim off any surface scum. Allow to settle for 10 minutes before spooning into warmed, sterilized jars. Seal when cool.
MAKES ABOUT 4 CUPS

# TANGERINE CONSERVE

*Serve Tangerine Conserve over ice cream or pound cake.*

INGREDIENTS
*8 firm tangerines or mandarins*
*3 cups (750 mL) water*
*5 cups (2½ pounds/1.25 kg) white granulated sugar, warmed*

*RIGHT: Whenever I look at this photograph of Whiskey Tangelo Marmalade, I'm reminded of why I love making preserves.*

Peel the fruit and reserve the peel. Cut the fruit in half, removing and reserving the seeds. Place the fruit in a food processor or a blender and pulverize. Transfer the pulp to a jam pan or a large, wide saucepan and add the water. Cut the peel into thin strips, enough to fill 1 cup, and add it to the pan with the warmed sugar. Place the pan over medium heat and stir until the sugar dissolves. Increase the heat and bring the conserve to a boil. Boil rapidly until setting point is reached, about 30 minutes. Ladle the jam into warmed, sterilized jars and seal.
MAKES ABOUT 4 CUPS

# Summer Berries

*Here the currants red and white*

*In yon green bush at her sight*

*Peep through their shady leaves and cry*

*Come eat me, as she passes by.*

ROBERT HEATH

LEFT: *Inspiration for preserve-making—a bowl of strawberries, blackberries, red currants, blueberries, and raspberries.*

# STRAWBERRY JAM

*A true classic, strawberry jam is the perfect accompaniment to morning toast.*

INGREDIENTS
*4 pounds (2 kg) firm, just under-ripe strawberries, hulled*
*Juice and zest of 3 oranges, seeds reserved*
*8 cups (4 pounds/2 kg) white granulated sugar, warmed*
*1 tablespoon butter*

Place the strawberries in a jam pan or a large, wide saucepan. Add the orange juice and zest. Place any seeds in a muslin bag, and attach it to the handle, allowing the bag to fall into the jam. Place the pan over low heat, bring the mixture to a boil, and simmer gently, covered, for 15 to 20 minutes or until the strawberries are very soft and pulpy. Mash them lightly with a potato masher. Squeeze the bag of seeds against the side of the pan to extract the pectin and then discard the bag. Add the warmed sugar to the pan and stir until it dissolves. Turn up the heat, and boil rapidly for 10 minutes or until setting point is reached. Remove the pan from the heat. Stir in the butter and lift off any surface scum. Leave for 10 minutes, stir well, then ladle the jam into warmed, sterilized jars. Seal the jars while the jam is hot. The jam is ready to eat immediately.

MAKES ABOUT 3 TO 4 CUPS

# BERRY CONSERVE

*A wonderful-looking conserve with whole berries suspended in a delicious syrup.*

INGREDIENTS
*1 cup (8 ounces/250 g) ripe strawberries or raspberries*
*Juice and zest of 1 lemon*
*White granulated sugar*

Weigh equal quantities of berries and sugar and place them in layers in a bowl, beginning with the berries and finishing with the sugar. Leave the bowl in a cool place, covered, for 24 hours. The next day, place the contents of the bowl in a jam pan or a large, wide saucepan, add the lemon juice and zest, and boil over high heat for 5 minutes. Set aside. The next day, reboil the conserve for 5 minutes and set aside. On the third day, reboil it for 8 minutes and then ladle carefully into warmed, sterilized jars and seal.

MAKES ABOUT 1 CUP

# STRAWBERRY BRANDY

*When choosing berries, inspect the bottom of the basket to make sure the berries are not squashed or moldy. Berries are fragile and perishable so the sooner they are preserved the better. Remove the plastic wrap, loosen the berries, and refrigerate until cooking.*

### INGREDIENTS
*2 cups (1 pound/500 g) ripe strawberries*
*1¼ cups (8 ounces/250 g) superfine (caster) sugar*
*½ cup (125 mL) water*
*2½ cups (625 mL) brandy*

Hull the strawberries and discard any bruised fruit. Place the strawberries in a large, sterilized, screw-top jar and gently squash them with a wooden spoon. Put the sugar and water in a saucepan over medium heat, bring to a boil and simmer, stirring until the sugar dissolves. Allow to cool and then add the syrup to the strawberries in the jar. Add the brandy and seal the jar well. Keep the jar in the refrigerator for 3 days, giving it an occasional shake. Strain through a very fine sieve or a muslin-lined sieve and pour the strawberry brandy into sterilized, sealable bottles. Discard the fruit pulp left in the sieve. Store the brandy in a cool, dry place for 1 month before drinking.

MAKES ABOUT 4 CUPS

*BELOW: The cultivated strawberries we purchase today originated in America when a native North American strawberry was bred with one from Chile.*

# RASPBERRY JAM

*Raspberries set very well, unlike strawberries, so it makes great sense to conserve this summer fruit for cooler times.*

INGREDIENTS
*2 pounds (1 kg) fresh, firm, under-ripe raspberries*
*4 cups (2 pounds/1 kg) white granulated sugar, warmed*

Place the raspberries in a jam pan or a large, wide saucepan. Crush the berries lightly with a wooden spoon. Place the pan over low heat and cook until the fruit bubbles, stirring occasionally to prevent it from sticking to the pan. Add the warmed sugar and stir carefully until the sugar dissolves. Increase the heat, bring the jam to a boil, and cook without stirring for 10 minutes or until setting point is reached. Ladle the jam into warmed, sterilized jars and seal them while the jam is hot.
MAKES 2 TO 3 CUPS

# RASPBERRY VINEGAR

*The method used here is not dissimilar to that used to make fruit jelly. The fruit and the liquid are strained through muslin without pressing the fruit so that the liquid stays clear. Pressing the fruit causes the liquid to go cloudy. Other berries can be used, such as blackberries, strawberries, and mulberries.*

INGREDIENTS
*1 cup (8 ounces/250 g) raspberries*
*2 cups (500 mL) white wine vinegar*

Place the berries in a glass bowl and crush them lightly with a potato masher. Reserve a few whole raspberries to use as decoration. Add the vinegar and cover the bowl with a clean dishcloth. Set the bowl aside in a warm place for 2 days.

Line a sieve with muslin and strain the crushed fruit and vinegar. Do not press the fruit to gain extra juice. Discard the crushed fruit. Pour the vinegar into sterilized bottles, add some fresh raspberries for decoration, and seal. This vinegar can be used immediately or stored in a cool, dark place for up to 6 months.
MAKES ABOUT 3 CUPS

*RIGHT: The fragile elegance of Raspberry Jam.*

*RIGHT: Raspberries and sugar, soon to be transformed into delectable Mixed Berry Jam.*

# MIXED BERRY JAM

*This is one of my favorite jams to eat on bitter cold days with hot scones and thick cream.*

INGREDIENTS
*2 large, firm green apples*
*2 cups (1 pound/500 g) firm*
  *blueberries*
*2 cups (1 pound/500 g) firm*
  *strawberries*
*2 cups (1 pound/500 g) firm*
  *raspberries or blackberries*
*White granulated sugar*
*Juice of 2 lemons*

Peel, core, and grate the apples. Hull the berries. Weigh the prepared fruit and for every pound (500 g) of fruit, measure 1½ cups (12 ounces/375 g) of sugar.

Place the fruit and the sugar in a jam pan or a large, wide saucepan over medium heat. Stir gently until the sugar dissolves, add the lemon juice, then bring the mixture to a boil over high heat and cook until setting point is reached, about 40 to 60 minutes. Ladle the jam into warmed, sterilized jars and seal.

MAKES ABOUT 6 CUPS

# RED CURRANT JELLY

*Red currant jelly is best eaten with lamb or duck, spread on toast and croissants, added to cooked red cabbage, or made into Cumberland sauce.*

INGREDIENTS
*4 pounds (2 kg) ripe but
  unblemished red currants
2½ cups (625 mL) water
White granulated sugar*

Remove any stalks from the currants. Place the currants in a jam pan or a large, wide saucepan, and add the water. Bring the water to a boil over medium heat and simmer until the fruit is soft, about 45 minutes. Mash the currants with a potato masher and pour the mixture into a sterilized jelly bag. Allow to drip into a bowl for at least 12 hours or overnight. Do not squeeze the jelly bag. Discard the fruit pulp left in the bag.

Measure the juice into the cleaned pan and place over a low heat. For every 2½ cups juice add 2 cups (1 pound/ 500 g) sugar. Stir the sugar into the juice, stirring constantly until the sugar dissolves. Bring the mixture to a boil and boil rapidly until setting point is reached, about 10 to 15 minutes. Pour the jelly into warmed, sterilized jars and seal. The jelly can be eaten immediately.

MAKES ABOUT 4 TO 6 CUPS

# BLACK CURRANT JAM

*Currants—red, black, and white—never really sweeten so they are best preserved, especially as they have plenty of pectin.*

INGREDIENTS
*2 pounds (1 kg) ripe black
  currants, stalks removed
1¼ cups (310 mL) water or
  apple juice
7 cups (3½ pounds/1.75 kg)
  white granulated sugar,
  warmed
Juice of 1 lemon*

Place the currants in a jam pan or a large, wide saucepan, add the water, and cook over medium heat for 10 minutes. Add the warmed sugar and stir constantly until the sugar dissolves. Add the lemon juice, turn up the heat, and bring the mixture to a boil. Cook the jam rapidly until setting point is reached, about 30 minutes. Ladle the jam into warmed, sterilized jars and seal.

MAKES ABOUT 4 CUPS

# BLUEBERRY JAM

*I like to eat this jam stirred through plain yogurt or cream for a quick dessert.*

INGREDIENTS
*2 pounds (1 kg) firm
   blueberries*
*Juice of 2 lemons*
*1¼ cups (310 mL) water*
*3 cups (1½ pounds/750 g) white
   granulated sugar, warmed*

Pick over the blueberries and discard any that are soft or bruised. Make sure the weight equals 2 pounds (1 kg). Place half the blueberries in a jam pan or a large, wide saucepan and squash the berries lightly with a wooden spoon. Add the lemon juice and water. Bring the mixture to a boil over medium heat and cook for 10 minutes. Add the warmed sugar and stir constantly until the sugar dissolves. Turn up the heat and boil until setting point is reached, about 30 minutes. Ladle the jam into warmed, sterilized jars and seal.
MAKES ABOUT 4 CUPS

# BLACKBERRY LIQUEUR

*This drink is said to be medicinal as well as enjoyable. It's excellent for soothing sore throats! Blackberries are exceptionally high in vitamin C. Although blackberry bushes are considered a noxious weed in subtropical areas, I still love to venture forth with a bucket to gather a summer's day harvest to preserve.*

INGREDIENTS
*4 pounds (2 kg) ripe
   blackberries*
*6 cups (3 pounds/1.5 kg) white
   granulated sugar*
*About 3 cups (750 mL) gin*

*RIGHT: A dish of blueberries
waiting for inspiration—
Blueberry Jam or enjoyed fresh
with clotted cream?*

Place the blackberries and the sugar in a basin in a warm place, such as beside a stove or a hot-water heater, until the juice is drawn from the berries, about 6 to 8 hours. Strain the juice through a jelly bag or a muslin-lined colander. Discard the berries. Measure the juice and add equal amounts of gin to juice. Mix well together, pour the blackberry liqueur into sterilized bottles, and seal. Store the liqueur in a cool, dark place.
MAKES ABOUT 4 TO 6 CUPS

# CRANBERRY AND APPLE JELLY

*Acidic cranberries make glorious jellies and jams to use in tarts, glazes, and pies.
Cranberry sauce was first invented by Native Americans, who sweetened the berries with
maple sugar or honey. Cranberries are still a most appreciated flavor with poultry.*

INGREDIENTS
4 pounds (2 kg) ripe green
  apples
3 pounds (1.5 kg) firm
  cranberries
Water
White granulated sugar

Roughly chop the apples (no need to peel or core them).
Place the apples and the cranberries in a jam pan or a large,
wide saucepan and just cover with cold water. Place the
saucepan over medium heat and cook until the apples are
soft, about 5 to 10 minutes. Ladle the fruit into a clean jelly
bag and allow it to drip overnight into a clean bowl.

The next day, measure the juice and return it to the pan.
Discard the fruit pulp left in the bag. For every 2½ cups
(625 mL) juice add 2 cups (1 pound/500 g) sugar to the pan.
Place the pan over high heat and stir constantly until the
sugar dissolves. Allow the mixture to boil until setting point
is reached, about 30 minutes. Ladle the jelly into warmed,
sterilized jars and seal.

MAKES ABOUT 6 TO 8 CUPS

# CRANBERRY GIN

*Cranberry gin, preserved in the summer months, makes a warming drink by the fire in the
depth of winter.*

INGREDIENTS
1 pound (500 g) ripe
  cranberries
1½ cups (11 ounces/340 g)
  superfine (caster) sugar
3 cups (750 mL) gin

Place the cranberries in a large, sterilized jar with a tight-
fitting lid. Add the sugar and the gin, seal, and shake gently.
Store in a dark place for 3 months, shaking the jar daily for
the first month and then weekly after that. Strain the liquid
through a fine mesh sieve or a muslin-lined sieve. Discard
the fruit pulp left in the sieve. Pour the cranberry gin into a
sterilized bottle and seal. Store in a cool, dark place.

MAKES ABOUT 3 TO 4 CUPS

# GOOSEBERRY CHUTNEY

*Gooseberries are a lovely yellow summer berry. After you have eaten some fresh, make the rest into a pot of chutney. This chutney is a delicious accompaniment to turkey, chicken, pork, or fish.*

INGREDIENTS

2 pounds (1 kg) gooseberries
1 onion, finely chopped
1½ cups (8 ounces/250 g)
  raisins
4½ cups (1½ pounds/750 g)
  brown sugar
2½ cups (625 mL) malt vinegar
1 teaspoon sea salt
1 teaspoon ground ginger
½ teaspoon cayenne pepper

Trim the gooseberries. Place all the ingredients in a nonreactive pan and bring the mixture slowly to a boil over low heat, stirring constantly until the sugar dissolves. Reduce the heat to a simmer and cook for about 1 hour, stirring occasionally, until the chutney thickens. Pour the chutney into warmed, sterilized jars. Seal the jars when the chutney has cooled.

MAKES ABOUT 4 CUPS

# GOOSEBERRY JAM

*Gooseberries make an excellent fruit jam. They often taste better preserved than fresh, unless you can get the fully ripe, large dessert variety, which are delicious when fresh.*

INGREDIENTS

2 pounds (1 kg) gooseberries
1¼ cups (310 mL) water
5 cups (2½ pounds/1.25 kg)
  white granulated sugar,
  warmed
Juice of 1 lemon

Remove and discard the dry gooseberry stalks. Place the gooseberries in a jam pan or a large, wide saucepan, add the water, and cook over medium heat until the gooseberries are just tender, about 10 minutes. Add the warmed sugar and lemon juice and keep stirring until the sugar dissolves. Turn up the heat, bring the mixture to a boil, and continue to cook rapidly until setting point is reached, about 45 minutes. Ladle the jam into warmed, sterilized jars and seal.

MAKES ABOUT 4 CUPS

# Luscious Stonefruit

So we grew together,

Like to a double cherry, seeming parted,

But yet an union in partition;

Two lovely berries moulded on one stem.

WILLIAM SHAKESPEARE

LEFT: *The best plums for preserves taste acidic and are not too juicy. Among those shown here are burbank, red ace, damson, and satsuma plums.*

47

# PEACHES IN BRANDY

*The white-fleshed peaches have the most flavor and tend to be more tender and juicy than the yellow variety.*

INGREDIENTS

*2 pounds (1 kg) firm, ripe,
small peaches or enough to fit
a large jar*

*2 cups (1 pound/500 g) white
granulated sugar*

*5 cups (1.25 liters) water*

*1 vanilla bean*

*About 3 cups (750 mL) brandy*

Place the peaches in a saucepan of boiling water and blanch for 3 to 4 minutes to soften the skins. Remove the peaches with a slotted spoon and when cool enough to handle, slip off the skins. When the peaches are cool, pack them into a large, sterilized jar. Make a syrup with the sugar, water, and the vanilla bean. Bring the mixture to a boil and continue boiling for 10 minutes. Cool and pour equal amounts of the syrup and the brandy over the peaches. Seal securely and store the peaches in a cool, dark place. Leave for 2 to 4 weeks before eating. They will keep for up to 6 months. MAKES 1 4-CUP JAR

# PEACH AND PASSION FRUIT JAM

*Some peaches cling to the stone, hence the name clingstone peaches, while with freestone varieties the flesh comes away easily.*

INGREDIENTS

*3 pounds (1.5 kg) fresh ripe
peaches, peeled, pitted, and
sliced*

*6 cups (3 pounds/1.5 kg) white
granulated sugar, warmed*

*Juice of 1 lemon*

*10 fresh passion fruits, puréed*

*RIGHT: Peaches in Brandy is
one of my all-time favorite
desserts.*

Place the peaches in a bowl and sprinkle with half the warmed sugar. Cover and leave to macerate overnight. The next day, place the contents of the bowl in a jam pan or a large, wide saucepan and bring to a boil. Lower the heat to a simmer and cook until the peaches are tender, about 15 minutes. Add the remaining warmed sugar, the lemon juice, and the passion fruit purée. Bring the mixture back to a boil and boil until setting point is reached, about 45 minutes to 1½ hours. Ladle the jam into warmed, sterilized jars and seal. MAKES ABOUT 4 CUPS

# SPICED PEACHES

*Clingstone peaches are best for this recipe because they hold their shape better than freestone varieties.*

INGREDIENTS
*4 cups (2 pounds/1 kg) white
   granulated sugar
3 cups (750 mL) malt vinegar
Peel and juice of 1 lemon
6 cloves
6 allspice berries
¾ inch (2 cm) piece fresh ginger
1 cinnamon stick, broken
4 pounds (2 kg) firm peaches,
   peeled, halved, and pitted*

Place the sugar and the vinegar in a large, nonreactive pan over low heat and stir until the sugar dissolves. Tie the lemon peel, cloves, allspice berries, ginger, and cinnamon stick into a muslin bag and add it to the pan. Place the lemon juice and 4 cups (1 liter) water in a bowl. Drop the peaches into the lemon water to prevent discoloration. Drain and rinse the peach halves in cold water and add them to the pan. Simmer over medium heat for 15 to 20 minutes or until the peaches are just tender. Remove the peaches carefully with a slotted spoon and arrange them in warmed, sterilized jars. Boil the sugar syrup rapidly for 10 minutes to thicken it and then pour it over the peaches. When cool, seal the jars. Store for 3 months before opening the jars.
MAKES ABOUT 2 8-CUP JARS

# PEACH CHUTNEY

*Serve this chutney on grilled game hen or chicken.*

INGREDIENTS
*2 pounds (1 kg) ripe peaches
2½ cups (13 ounces/405 g)
   brown sugar
¾ cup (4 ounces/125 g) raisins
2 cloves garlic, chopped
2 tablespoons grated ginger
1 red chile (chilli), chopped
1 onion, chopped
1 teaspoon sea salt
1¼ cups (310 mL) white wine
   vinegar*

Peel, pit, and chop the peaches. Place them in a large nonreactive saucepan over medium heat and add the remaining ingredients. Stir for 5 minutes and when the mixture is boiling, lower the heat to a simmer and cook for 30 to 40 minutes until the chutney thickens. Ladle the chutney into warmed, sterilized jars. Allow to cool and then seal the jars. The chutney is ready to eat after 1 month.
MAKES ABOUT 4 CUPS

*RIGHT: The peaches we cultivate today are not very different from the peaches eaten by the Romans, Chinese, Indians, and Persians two to three thousand years ago.*

# CHERRY CHUTNEY

*Sour cherries, the most famous of which is the juicy black morello, make excellent chutneys.*

INGREDIENTS

2 pounds (1 kg) dark, ripe but
  unblemished cherries
2½ cups (12 ounces/375 g)
  golden raisins (sultanas)
½ cup (125 mL) white vinegar
1 cup (5 ounces/155 g) brown
  sugar
½ teaspoon ground ginger
1 teaspoon allspice (mixed
  spice)

Halve and pit the cherries. Place them in a large, nonreactive saucepan and add the other ingredients. Stir over low heat until the sugar dissolves, then bring the mixture to a boil, increase the heat, and cook for 3 to 5 minutes. Reduce the heat and simmer until the chutney thickens, about 20 minutes. Ladle the chutney into warmed, sterilized jars, cool, and then seal.

MAKES ABOUT 3 CUPS

# CHERRY JELLY

*Take care to choose ripe, unblemished cherries for this recipe.*

INGREDIENTS

3 pounds (1.5 kg) ripe, dark
  cherries, stalked, halved, and
  pitted
½ cup (125 mL) water
Juice of 1 lemon
White granulated sugar,
  warmed
4 tablespoons powdered citrus
  pectin

Place the cherries in a jam pan or a large, wide saucepan and mash them with a potato masher. Add the water and lemon juice. Place the pan over medium heat, bring to a boil, and simmer for 20 minutes. Ladle the mixture into a sterilized jelly bag and leave it to drip into a bowl overnight.

The next day, measure the juice and for every cup of liquid put aside 1 cup (8 ounces/250 g) sugar. Discard the fruit pulp left in the bag. Place the juice in the cleaned pan and mix in the citrus pectin. Place the pan over high heat and bring the juice to a boil, stirring constantly. When the juice is boiling, add the warmed sugar, reduce the heat, and stir until the sugar dissolves. Turn up the heat, bring the jelly back to a rapid boil, and cook it until setting point is reached, about 30 minutes. Ladle the jelly into warmed, sterilized jars and seal.

MAKES ABOUT 4 CUPS

# CHERRIES IN GRAPPA

*Drain and dip the cherries in melted dark chocolate to serve with strong black coffee.*

INGREDIENTS
*2 pounds (1 kg) best quality,
   firm, dark cherries
6 white granulated sugar cubes,
   crushed
Grappa, brandy, or kirsch*

Snip half of the stalk off each cherry, leaving some on for handling and as an attractive touch when serving. Prick over each cherry with a fine needle. Pack the cherries into sterilized jars and between each layer of cherries add some crushed sugar. Cover the fruit with grappa and seal well, making sure the jars are absolutely airtight. Leave the cherries in a cool, dark place to mature for 6 months.
MAKES ABOUT 4 CUPS

# CHERRY JAM

*Cherries will keep refrigerated for a few days, but use them immediately for the best results.*

INGREDIENTS
*6 pounds (3 kg) dark cherries
12 cups (6 pounds/3 kg) white
   granulated sugar
Juice of 2 lemons
Fine zest of 1 lemon*

Remove the cherry stalks. Cut the cherries in half and remove the stones. Place the cherries in a jam pan or a large, wide saucepan with the sugar, lemon juice, and zest. Bring the mixture to a boil over medium heat and stir until the sugar dissolves. Turn up the heat and boil until setting point is reached, about 40 minutes. Remove the pan from the heat and leave it to stand for 10 minutes. Stir the jam well and then ladle it into warmed, sterilized jars and seal.
MAKES ABOUT 8 CUPS

---

### CHERRIES

There are many varieties of cherry — large sweet black, acid sweet red, pale cream, heart-shaped — and all can be used for different kinds of preserves. Whatever color or shape, when buying, look for plump fruit, clean, glossy, and unbroken skins, and fresh green stalks. Look them over carefully to avoid bruised ones.

# APRICOT AND CARDAMOM CHUTNEY

*I make it a policy to always use fresh spices and to buy them in small quantities from a supplier with a large turnover. A cardamom pod in peak condition is pale green, not a dried straw color.*

INGREDIENTS

*2 pounds (1 kg) ripe apricots, halved, pitted, and quartered*

*1½ cups (12 ounces/375 g) raw (demerara) sugar*

*1 teaspoon ground cardamom*

*1 teaspoon grated fresh ginger*

*½ teaspoon ground allspice*

*½ teaspoon ground cinnamon*

*½ teaspoon ground cloves*

*1 fresh, small red chile (chilli), seeded and chopped*

*1 large onion, chopped*

*1 cup (6 ounces/185 g) raisins*

*¼ cup (1 ounce/30 g) sunflower seeds*

*2 cups (500 mL) white wine vinegar*

Place all the ingredients in a large, nonreactive saucepan over high heat and bring the mixture to a boil, stirring continuously. Reduce the heat to a simmer and cook until the chutney thickens, about 30 minutes, depending on the ripeness of the apricots. Ladle the chutney into warmed, sterilized jars, cool, and then seal. Store the chutney in a cool, dark place. Leave for 4 weeks before opening.

MAKES ABOUT 5 CUPS

---

APRICOTS

Apricots for jam, chutney, or sweet preserves should always be ripe when bought as they won't mature and sweeten after they are picked. When buying, feel the fruit; it should be just soft with an orange flush. Keep the ripe fruit refrigerated until using it. If you have a windfall of unripe apricots they can be cooked into delicious pickles and chutneys.

---

*RIGHT: Apricot and Cardamom Chutney has a Middle-Eastern flavor that makes it perfect to serve with a vegetable couscous.*

# FRESH APRICOT JAM

*Apricots vary in color from pale yellow to deep orange, with a red freckled skin, and they vary also in flavor. When making jam, ensure the apricots are ripe, sweet, and not floury, otherwise you will have gone to a lot of effort for an indifferent result.*

INGREDIENTS

*6 pounds (3 kg) fresh, firm apricots*

*12 cups (6 pounds/3 kg) white granulated sugar*

*1¼ cups (310 mL) water*

Halve and pit the apricots. Crack 12 of the pits and remove the kernels. Discard the remaining pits. Place the apricot halves in a bowl with the sugar and water and leave to stand overnight.

The next day, place the contents of the bowl in a jam pan or a large, wide saucepan and bring the mixture to a boil. At the same time, blanch the kernels in boiling water for 3 to 5 minutes and add them to the jam for the last 5 minutes of cooking. Allow the jam to boil over medium heat until setting point is reached, about 45 minutes. Stir the jam well and then ladle it into warmed, sterilized jars, and seal.

MAKES ABOUT 10 CUPS

*RIGHT: I delight in the range of colors in the skin and flesh of the different varieties of plum—from pale green to gold, red to purple, and dark blue to black. These are Burbank plums.*

# PLUM AND RAISIN CHUTNEY

*Serve this spicy chutney with hot or cold meats and cheese. Sweet eating plums such as Satsuma, Blood Plum, Greengage, Santa Rosa, and Burbank are eagerly looked for in late summer. They have a higher sugar content and a richer flavor than cooking plums. The best preserving plums, however, are acidic and tart, and not as pleasant to eat raw. I am lucky to have an oversupply of all varieties every year from my parents' country garden and I have great pleasure making them into jams, chutneys, pickles, and liqueurs.*

INGREDIENTS

4 pounds (2 kg) firm plums
1 pound (500 g) cooking apples
1 pound (500 g) onions
3 cloves garlic, finely chopped
3 tablespoons finely chopped
  fresh ginger
1½ cups (8 ounces/250 g)
  raisins
3 cups (1 pound/500 g) brown
  sugar
4 cups (1 liter) malt vinegar
1 tablespoon sea salt
1 teaspoon ground cloves
½ teaspoon ground cinnamon

Remove and discard the plum stalks. Chop the plums roughly and remove the pits. Peel, core, and chop the apples and the onions. Place all the ingredients in a nonreactive pan and cook over low heat, stirring, until the sugar dissolves. Bring the mixture to a boil, lower the heat to a simmer, and gently cook for 1½ to 2 hours or until setting point is reached. Stir occasionally to prevent sticking. Spoon the chutney into warmed, sterilized jars. Cover with a dishcloth and seal when cold. Keep the chutney for 3 to 4 months before opening.

MAKES ABOUT 6 CUPS

---

NATIVE AMERICAN PLUMS

Native American plums are still grown, as well as species derived from the native plums. These include Chickasaw, *Prunus Americana*, Oregon plum, and Texas plum. These native fruits are much hardier than the exotic kinds, and are better able to withstand the onslaught of pests, diseases, and extreme changes of weather.

# SPICED PICKLED PLUMS

*Serve these plums with cheese. They're especially fine with an aged Cheddar and cold lager.*

INGREDIENTS
*1 tablespoon mustard seeds*
*1 teaspoon whole peppercorns*
*1 bay leaf*
*2 cups (10 ounces/310 g)*
  *brown sugar*
*4 cups (1 liter) malt vinegar*
*1 teaspoon sea salt*
*5 pounds (2.5 kg) small red*
  *plums*
*Cinnamon sticks*
*Allspice berries*

Put the mustard seeds, peppercorns, and bay leaf into a muslin bag. Place the sugar, vinegar, salt, and the muslin bag in a saucepan over medium heat and bring the mixture to a boil. Reduce the heat and simmer for 10 minutes. Remove the saucepan from the heat and allow to cool. Discard the muslin bag. Return the saucepan to the heat and bring the mixture to a boil once again. Prick the plums 4 to 6 times with a needle and pack them into sterilized jars. Add a cinnamon stick and 6 allspice berries to each jar. Pour the hot, spiced vinegar over and seal. Store the plums in a cool, dark place for up to 6 months. The plums will be ready to eat after 4 to 6 weeks.

MAKES ABOUT 6 CUPS

---

PLUMS

Plums come in many shapes, colors, and flavors, the sweetest being the best for fresh eating and desserts. Save the smaller, bitter-skinned ones for making preserves. They are usually smaller and less juicy, and their acidity helps to make them more delicious when cooked. Plums will not keep for more than a few days so make sure you buy firm, unblemished ones and refrigerate until cooking.

---

*LEFT: These Spiced Pickled Plums have been made from small cherry plums. The plums are not very juicy eaten fresh, but really improve with cooking.*

# PLUM SAUCE

*This delicious sauce can be served with hot or cold chicken, duck, and pork.*

INGREDIENTS
4 pounds (2 kg) ripe plums
1 pound (500 g) onions,
  chopped
1¼ cups (310 mL) malt vinegar
1 teaspoon sea salt
1 teaspoon ground ginger
1 teaspoon allspice berries
1 teaspoon mustard seeds
1 fresh, small red chile (chilli),
  seeded and chopped
1½ cups (8 ounces/250 g)
  brown sugar
½ cup (3 ounces/90 g) golden
  raisins (sultanas)

Halve the plums and remove the pits. Roughly chop the flesh. Place the plums, onions, vinegar, salt, ginger, allspice berries, mustard seeds (lightly crushed), and chile in a nonreactive saucepan over medium heat. Bring the mixture to a boil, reduce the heat, and simmer for 30 minutes. Remove the saucepan from the heat and push the pulp through a sieve or drum grater. Return the liquid to the cleaned saucepan and add the sugar and golden raisins. Put the saucepan over medium heat until the mixture begins to boil, then lower the heat, and simmer, stirring occasionally, for 45 minutes or until the sauce has thickened. Pour the sauce into warmed, sterilized bottles, cool, and then seal. Store the plum sauce in a cool, dry place for up to 12 months. It is ready to use after 4 weeks.
MAKES ABOUT 6 TO 8 CUPS

# PLUM AND APPLE JAM

*This simple recipe is a wonderful way to take advantage of a bountiful supply of plums.*

INGREDIENTS
2 pounds (1 kg) firm plums
¼ cup (60 mL) water
1 pound (500 g) firm cooking
  apples, peeled, and chopped
6 cups (3 pounds/1.5 kg) white
  granulated sugar, warmed

RIGHT: Plum Sauce made from
a really old recipe of my
mother's.

Remove and discard the plum stalks. Cut the plums in half and remove the pits if possible. Leave them in if this is too difficult and remove them later. Place the cut plums in a jam pan or a large, wide saucepan, add the water, bring the water to a boil and simmer the plums until they are soft, about 10 minutes. Remove any pits, add the apples, and simmer for 15 minutes. Stir in the warmed sugar and boil rapidly until setting point is reached, about 30 minutes. Ladle the jam into warmed, sterilized jars and seal.
MAKES ABOUT 4 CUPS

# Apples, Pears, AND *Quinces*

A heap

Of candied apple, quince, and plum, and gourd:

With jellies soother than the creamy curd,

And lucent syrops tinct with cinnamon.

JOHN KEATS

LEFT: *Still life of home-grown pears.*

# APPLE GINGER JAM

*The delicate ginger flavor of this jam complements muffins and scones.*

INGREDIENTS
*4 pounds (2 kg) cooking apples,
  ripe but not bruised
1¼-inch (3 cm) piece fresh
  ginger
Rind of 2 lemons
2½ cups (625 mL) water
6 cups (3 pounds/1.5 kg) white
  granulated sugar, warmed
½ cup (125 mL) fresh lemon
  juice*

Peel, core, and quarter the apples, reserving the cores and peel. Peel and lightly bruise the piece of ginger. Place the apple cores and peel, ginger, and lemon rind in a muslin bag and tie it up with string. Place the apples, muslin bag, and water in a jam pan or a large, wide saucepan. Bring the water to a boil, reduce the heat, and simmer for 30 minutes or until the apples are soft and pulpy. Squeeze the muslin bag into the jam pan to extract the pectin. Discard the bag. Add the warmed sugar and cook over low heat, stirring until the sugar dissolves. Stir in the lemon juice and bring the mixture to a boil. Turn up the heat and boil rapidly for 20 minutes or until setting point is reached. Skim off any scum if necessary. Allow the jam to stand for 10 minutes, then ladle it into sterilized jars and seal. The jam is ready to eat immediately.
MAKES ABOUT 6 CUPS

# APPLE AND DATE SALSA

*This salsa will keep for weeks in the refrigerator. Serve it with chicken or pork dishes.*

INGREDIENTS
*2 pounds (1 kg) green apples
8 ounces (250 g) onions
3 cups (1 pound/500 g) soft
  dried dates
4½ cups (1½ pounds/750 g)
  moist brown sugar
2 teaspoons ground allspice
1 teaspoon sea salt
½ teaspoon white pepper*

Peel, core, and quarter the apples. Peel and quarter the onions. Grind the dates, apples, and onions in a grinder (mincer) or food processor and transfer the mixture to a bowl. Add the remaining ingredients and mix well. Ladle the salsa into sterilized jars, seal, and store in the refrigerator for several weeks.
MAKES ABOUT 2 CUPS

*RIGHT: Apple Ginger Jam has a subtle ginger flavor. Serve it on warm scones with thick cream.*

# APPLE AND GERANIUM JELLY

*Just a few geranium leaves add an intense flavor to this jelly.*

INGREDIENTS

*4 pounds (2 kg) firm cooking
  apples, roughly chopped
12 rose or spiced geranium
  leaves, washed
4 cups (1 liter) water
White granulated sugar
Juice of 1 lemon*

Place the apple and the geranium leaves in a jam pan or a large, wide saucepan, add the water, bring to a boil and simmer until the apple is very soft, about 5 to 10 minutes. Discard the geranium leaves. Ladle the pulp into a jelly bag and allow it to drip into a bowl overnight. Discard the fruit pulp left in the bag. The next day, measure the juice and for every cup (250 mL) juice add 1 cup (8 ounces/250 g) sugar. Place the juice and the sugar in the cleaned pan with the lemon juice over medium heat, stirring until the sugar dissolves. Increase the heat and boil rapidly until setting point is reached, about 30 to 40 minutes. Ladle the jelly into warmed, sterilized jars and seal.

MAKES ABOUT 6 CUPS

# SPICY APPLE CHUTNEY

*Surprising spicy flavors — chiles, pepper, and ginger — enliven this chutney.*

INGREDIENTS

*2 pounds (1 kg) cooking apples
2 large onions
2 small, red chiles (chillies)
3 cups brown sugar
2 teaspoons ground allspice
2 teaspoons ground cloves
1 teaspoon sea salt
½ teaspoon black pepper
2 tablespoons chopped ginger
3 cups (750 mL) cider vinegar*

Peel, core, and chop the apples. Peel and finely chop the onions. Seed and slice the chiles. Place all the ingredients in a nonreactive pan, bring the mixture to a boil, and cook over medium heat for about 30 to 40 minutes or until the mixture thickens. Stir occasionally to prevent it from sticking. Ladle into warmed, sterilized jars and seal when cold.

MAKES ABOUT 4 TO 6 CUPS

*RIGHT: A gift of apples from a friendly neighbor. She prefers gardening so I make the apple jellies and chutneys for both of us.*

# APPLE AND PLUM CHUTNEY

*Unripe apples are very acidic, and full of flavor and pectin, making them perfect for preserving. Look out for windfalls and gluts in the market. Any variety of plum can be used in this recipe, so choose whatever is in season.*

## INGREDIENTS

*2 pounds (1 kg) firm green apples*
*4 pounds (2 kg) plums*
*1 pound (500 g) onions*
*2 cloves garlic*
*2 cups (10 ounces/ 310 g) golden raisins (sultanas)*
*2 cups (500 mL) white wine vinegar*
*3 cups (1 pound/500 g) moist brown sugar*
*2 teaspoons sea salt*
*1 teaspoon ground allspice*
*1 teaspoon ground ginger*
*½ teaspoon ground nutmeg*
*¼ teaspoon ground cloves*
*¼ teaspoon freshly ground black pepper*
*1 tablespoon mustard seeds*

Peel, core, and dice the apples and place them in a large nonreactive pan. Halve, pit, and dice the plums and add them to the pan. Peel and chop the onions and garlic and add to the pan with the remaining ingredients. Place the pan over medium heat and stir for 5 minutes. Bring the mixture to a boil and then simmer, uncovered, until the chutney thickens, about 1½ hours. Ladle it into warmed, sterilized jars, cool, and then seal.

MAKES ABOUT 6 CUPS

---

### APPLES

Apples have been grown for over three thousand years and until the twentieth century the apple was almost the only fruit available through the winter months. The earliest English apples were introduced from Europe and from them were bred favorite apples such as Cox's Orange Pippin. When America and Australia were settled by Europeans, new varieties were bred, such as the hardy Granny Smith. Some of these new apple varieties then found their way back to Europe.

---

*LEFT: Apple and Plum Chutney is a delicious, sweet-tasting chutney that is perfect to serve with a variety of cold meats.*

# APPLE CHUTNEY

*Choose firm green apples — mealy ones will ruin the texture of the chutney.*

INGREDIENTS
*2 pounds (1 kg) apples*
*2 large onions*
*¾-inch (2 cm) piece fresh ginger*
*3 cups (1 pound/500 g) moist*
  *brown sugar*
*1 teaspoon ground cloves*
*1 teaspoon ground allspice*
*2 teaspoons mustard seeds*
*3 cups (750 mL) cider vinegar*
*1¼ cups (5 ounces/155 g)*
  *toasted walnuts*

Peel, core, and chop the apples. Peel and chop the onions. Finely chop the ginger. Place all the ingredients except for the walnuts in a large, nonreactive saucepan. Bring the mixture to a boil over medium heat, then reduce the heat and simmer until the chutney thickens, about 45 to 60 minutes. Stir in the walnuts, and keep stirring for 5 minutes. Ladle the chutney into warmed, sterilized jars, cool, and seal.
MAKES ABOUT 4 CUPS

# CRAB APPLE JELLY

*Tart crab apple jelly is wonderful with any type of roasted poultry.*

INGREDIENTS
*2 pounds (1 kg) firm crab*
  *apples, stalks removed*
*Water*
*White granulated sugar*
*Juice of 1 lemon*

Cut the crab apples in half and place them in a jam pan or a large, wide saucepan. Pour in enough water to just cover the fruit. Place the saucepan over medium heat, bring the water to a boil, and cook the crab apples until they are soft, about 5 minutes. Ladle them into a jelly bag and leave to drip undisturbed into a bowl overnight. Discard the fruit pulp left in the bag. The next day, measure the liquid into a jam pan or a large, wide saucepan and for every cup (250 mL) liquid, add 1 cup (8 ounces/250 g) sugar. Stir in the lemon juice. Place the pan over medium heat and bring the mixture to a boil, stirring to dissolve the sugar. Allow the jelly to boil until setting point is reached, about 40 minutes. Ladle the jelly into warmed, sterilized jars, cool, and then seal.
MAKES ABOUT 4 CUPS

# PICKLED PEARS

*Tiny pink and green corella pears are ideal to pickle, and they look interesting on an antipasto platter. Larger, quartered pears can be used instead.*

INGREDIENTS
*20 corella pears or 5 large pears*
*1 tablespoon cider vinegar*
*4 cups (2 pounds/1 kg) white granulated sugar*
*1¼ cups (310 mL) cider vinegar*
*2 teaspoons cloves*
*2 teaspoons allspice berries*
*3 cinnamon sticks*
*1 tablespoon slivered fresh ginger*

*BELOW: Boxes of pears at the local market—plentiful and inexpensive.*

Peel the pears and, if using the large pears, cut them into quarters. Plunge the pears immediately into a bowl of water with the tablespoon of vinegar added. Place the sugar and the 1¼ cups cider vinegar in a nonreactive pan over low heat, stirring occasionally until the sugar dissolves. Tie the cloves, allspice berries, cinnamon sticks, and ginger into a muslin bag. Add the bag to the sweetened vinegar. Drain the pears and add them to the vinegar mixture. Turn up the heat to medium and boil until the pears are just tender, about 10 minutes. Remove the pan from the heat, discard the muslin bag, lift the pears out with a slotted spoon, and transfer them to warmed, sterilized jars, packing them down well. Return the vinegar mixture to the heat and continue to boil for 10 minutes or until it thickens. Pour the hot vinegar over the pears and seal the jars. Store the pears in a cool, dark place for 1 month before opening. The pears will keep for 6 to 12 months.
MAKES 1 8-CUP JAR

# PEAR AND GINGER MARMALADE

*Pears are second only to apples in popularity, though they are harder to grow. Any variety of pear that is green when ripe is the best to cook and preserve with.*

INGREDIENTS
*6 pounds (3 kg) ripe pears*
*2 cups (500 mL) apple cider*
*Juice of 2 lemons*
*Zest of 1 lemon*
*½ cup (3 ounces/90 g) preserved ginger, finely chopped*
*8 cups (4 pounds/2 kg) white granulated sugar, warmed*

Peel, core, and roughly chop the pears. Place them in a jam pan or a large, wide saucepan, add the apple cider, bring to a boil, and simmer until the pears are soft, about 10 minutes. Push the pears through a sieve and return the pulp to the pan with the remaining ingredients. Bring the mixture to a boil over medium heat, stirring constantly until the sugar dissolves. Turn up the heat and boil rapidly until setting point is reached, about 30 to 40 minutes. Ladle the marmalade into warmed, sterilized jars and seal.
MAKES ABOUT 8 CUPS

# PEARS IN CALVADOS

*Keep a jar or two of these pears handy — they make a great dessert.*

INGREDIENTS
*3 pounds (1.5 kg) slightly under-ripe pears*
*1 cup (8 ounces/250 g) white granulated sugar*
*2¼ cups (575 mL) water*
*Juice and zest of 2 fresh limes*
*2 star anise*
*1 small cinnamon stick*
*6 allspice berries*
*2¼ cups (575 mL) Calvados*

Peel, core, and halve the pears. Place the sugar and water in a saucepan over low heat and stir until the sugar dissolves. Add the pear halves, lime juice, spices, and zest and simmer for 10 minutes. Allow to cool. Lift out the pears with a slotted spoon, pack them into sterilized jars, and add enough Calvados to cover. Seal well and store the pears in a cool pantry.
MAKES ABOUT 8 CUPS

*RIGHT: The best pears have buttery flesh, and are slightly acidic yet sweet, with a strong, fragrant perfume. Pear and Ginger Marmalade was made from a glut of corella pears.*

# PEAR APRICOT JAM

*Try this easy-to-make jam on whole-wheat muffins or toast.*

INGREDIENTS

*3 pounds (1.5 kg) firm pears,
  peeled, cored, and chopped*
*Juice and zest of 2 firm lemons*
*2½ cups (625 mL) water*
*2½ cups (10 ounces/310 g) soft
  dried apricots*
*4 cups (2 pounds/1 kg) white
  granulated sugar, warmed*

Place the pears in a jam pan or a large, wide saucepan and cover with the lemon juice, zest, and water. Chop the apricots and add them to the pan. Place the pan over medium heat, bring the mixture to a boil, and simmer until the pears are soft, about 10 minutes. Add the warmed sugar and cook over low heat, stirring well, until the sugar dissolves. Increase the heat and boil rapidly for about 20 to 30 minutes until setting point is reached. Skim off any surface scum and leave for 10 minutes. Ladle the jam into warmed, sterilized jars and seal when cool.

MAKES ABOUT 4 CUPS

# PEAR AND CRANBERRY CHUTNEY

*Sweet pears and tart cranberries are a winning combination.*

INGREDIENTS

*2 pounds (1 kg) firm pears*
*6 ounces (185 g) onions*
*13 ounces (405 g) canned
  cranberry sauce*
*1½ cups (7 ounces/225 g) moist
  brown sugar*
*½ teaspoon ground ginger*
*½ teaspoon ground allspice*
*½ teaspoon ground cloves*
*½ teaspoon white pepper*
*1 teaspoon sea salt*
*2½ cups (625 mL) cider vinegar*

Peel, core, and dice the pears. Peel and chop the onions. Place all the ingredients in a nonreactive saucepan over medium heat and stir for 10 minutes. Bring the mixture to a boil, then reduce the heat and simmer the chutney, uncovered, for about 1 hour or until the chutney thickens. Ladle it into warmed, sterilized jars, leave to cool, then seal well. Store the chutney in a cool, dark place.

MAKES ABOUT 4 CUPS

*RIGHT: Pear Apricot Jam was made from Packham pears, which are ideal for preserving. They are a hard pear with less flavor than some of the other varieties, but they keep well so it is worthwhile buying in bulk.*

# PEAR CHUTNEY

*Serve this chutney with roasted chicken or turkey.*

INGREDIENTS
*6 pounds (3 kg) ripe pears*
*4 pounds (2 kg) ripe tomatoes*
*2 firm green apples*
*2 large onions*
*1 teaspoon sea salt*
*1 teaspoon ground ginger*
*1 teaspoon ground allspice*
*1 teaspoon cayenne pepper*
*4 cups (1 liter) white wine*
  *vinegar*
*10 cups (5 pounds/2.5 kg)*
  *moist brown sugar*

Peel, core, and chop the pears. Blanch the tomatoes in boiling water to remove the skins and then chop them roughly. Peel, core, and chop the apples. Chop the onions. Place all the ingredients in a large, nonreactive pan over medium heat and stir until the sugar dissolves. Allow the mixture to simmer steadily until the chutney thickens to setting point, about 1½ to 2 hours. Ladle it into warmed, sterilized jars, allow to cool, and then seal.
MAKES ABOUT 12 CUPS

# QUINCE BUTTER

*When shopping for quinces, look for firm fruit with a deep yellow color.*

INGREDIENTS
*2 pounds (1 kg) firm ripe*
  *quinces, washed and roughly*
  *chopped*
*White granulated sugar*
*Juice of 1 lemon*
*Butter*

Place the quinces in a jam pan or a large, wide saucepan with just enough water to cover the fruit. Bring the water to a boil, then simmer over medium heat until the quinces are very soft and pulpy, about 45 minutes. Push the pulp through a sieve. Measure the pulp back into the pan and for every cup of pulp add ¾ cup (6 ounces/185 g) sugar. Add the lemon juice and place the pan over medium heat, stirring until the sugar dissolves. Stir in 3 tablespoons of butter for each cup of pulp. Simmer, uncovered, until thick, about 20 to 30 minutes. Take care at this stage as the mixture bubbles and spits and can cause a nasty burn. Ladle the quince butter into warmed, sterilized jars, allow it to cool a little, and then seal. Store in a cool, dry place. Refrigerate after opening.
MAKES ABOUT 4 CUPS

# QUINCE JELLY

*I remember, while living in the country as a child, waiting for quinces to ripen to enjoy with my school lunch. They were grown in many back gardens then and even though they seemed hard and rather dry they had some appeal. Maybe it was simply that they were only around for so short a time. They are more commonly preserved into jams, jellies, and confectionery, and turn a very pretty pink when cooked.*

INGREDIENTS
*4 pounds (2 kg) under-ripe*
  *quinces*
*White granulated sugar*

Wash the quinces and remove the fur. Chop them very roughly and place the fruit in a pan with enough cold water to just cover them. Bring the water to a boil over medium heat and cook the quinces until the fruit is very pulpy, about 45 minutes. Place the contents of the pan into a jelly bag and allow it to drip overnight; do not squeeze the bag or the jelly will be cloudy.

The next day, measure the juice and for each 1¼ cups (310 mL) juice add 1 cup (8 ounces/250 g) sugar. Discard the fruit pulp left in the bag. Boil the juice and sugar together for about 30 to 40 minutes or until setting point is reached. Remove any scum that rises to the surface. Spoon the jelly into warmed, sterilized jars and seal when cool.
MAKES ABOUT 6 CUPS

QUINCES

Quinces are distantly related to the same family as apples and pears and came originally from Anatolia in Turkey, and Iran. They can be made into wonderful jellies, pastes, jams, and sauces. Look out for them in deserted farmhouse orchards.

Unripe quinces are best for making into jelly, as they contain the most pectin. If the quinces are ripe, use equal quantities of firm, tart cooking apples and quinces to add pectin which will give a better jell.

# Grapes, Figs,
## AND Melons

Now sing of the fig, Simiane,

Because its loves are hidden.

I sing the fig, said she,

Whose beautiful loves are hidden,

Its flowering is folded away

Closed room where marriages are made:

No perfume tells the tale outside.

ANDRÉ GIDE

LEFT: *Figs grow prolifically in the gardens surrounding my home so I am often able to enjoy figs in perfect condition.*

# GRAPE JELLY

*Black grapes make a very dark jelly, while white grapes make a green to yellow jelly.*

INGREDIENTS

*3 pounds (1.5 kg) ripe grapes,
    stalks removed*
*2 pounds (1 kg) cooking apples,
    roughly chopped*
*1 lemon, sliced*
*6 cardamom pods*
*1¼ cups (310 mL) dry white
    wine*
*White granulated sugar*

Place the grapes, apples, lemon, cardamom pods, and wine in a jam pan or a large, wide saucepan, bring the mixture to a boil over medium heat, and cook for 30 minutes or until the fruit is soft and pulpy. Pour the mixture into a jelly bag placed over a large bowl and leave it to drip for 12 hours or overnight. Discard the fruit pulp left in the bag. Measure the juice into the cleaned jam pan and for every 2½ cups (625 mL) juice add 2 cups (1 pound/500 g) sugar. Place the pan over low heat and stir until the sugar dissolves. Increase the heat and boil for 10 minutes or until setting point is reached. Pour the jelly into warmed, sterilized jars and seal. The jelly will be ready in 2 weeks.

MAKES ABOUT 6 TO 8 CUPS

# GRAPE JAM

*Choose fresh, plump grapes for the best-tasting jam and wait 2 weeks before eating it.*

INGREDIENTS

*2 pounds (1 kg) firm, ripe
    white or black grapes, stems
    removed*
*2 cups (500 mL) water*
*½ cup (3 ounces/90 g) raisins*
*1 cup (250 mL) fresh orange
    juice*
*6 cups (3 pounds/1.5 kg) white
    granulated sugar, warmed*

To squeeze the pulp from the grapes, put them into a colander over a bowl and press them with a potato masher. Reserve the skins. Put the grape pulp and the water in a jam pan or a large, wide saucepan over low heat. Bring the mixture to a boil and simmer for 20 to 30 minutes. Remove the pan from the heat, skim off the seeds, and discard them. Add the skins, raisins, and orange juice to the pan. Place the pan over medium heat and bring the mixture to a boil. Reduce the heat and simmer for 20 minutes. Add the warmed sugar and stir until the sugar dissolves. Increase the heat and boil rapidly until the jam reaches setting point, about 30 minutes. Ladle the jam into warmed, sterilized jars and seal.

# GRAPES IN ARMAGNAC

*Armagnac is an aged brandy that was developed in the area around Armagnac in France. Try these grapes drained and added to a fruit salad or as an accompaniment to a bread and butter pudding.*

INGREDIENTS

*4½ cups (1½ pounds/750 g)
   moist brown sugar*
*2 cups (500 mL) water*
*6 cloves*
*2 cinnamon sticks*
*2 limes, sliced*
*3 cups grapes, stalks removed*
*2 tablespoons preserved ginger,
   finely sliced*
*About 2 to 3 cups
   (500–750 mL) Armagnac*

Place the sugar, water, cloves, cinnamon sticks, and lime slices in a large saucepan. Cook, stirring, over low heat until the sugar dissolves. Add the grapes and poach gently for 3 minutes. Remove the grapes with a slotted spoon and layer them in jars with the lime slices, ginger slices, and cinnamon sticks. Continue to boil the syrup until it is reduced a little, about 10 minutes. Add an equal quantity of Armagnac to syrup and fill the jars. Store for 4 weeks before opening and refrigerate after opening a jar.

MAKES ABOUT 1 4-CUP JAR

---

GRAPES

Many varieties of grape are grown for both wine making and eating. Grapes need to be fresh and ripe for grape juice, but unripe grapes are pressed for verjuice, a piquant juice that can be used in place of vinegar. Green or black muscat grapes, if you can get them, are best to use for preserving in alcohol.

When buying grapes, check that the fruits have unblemished skins with fresh, green stems. The fruits should be plump with no sign of wrinkling and there should be no shrivelled grapes on the stems.

---

# PICKLED GRAPES

*Choose unblemished muscatel grapes or large, firm black grapes. Serve with a platter of cold meats or cheese.*

INGREDIENTS
*2 pounds (1 kg) grapes*
*1 cup (250 mL) white wine vinegar*
*⅔ cup (5 ounces/155 g) white granulated sugar*
*1 teaspoon mustard seeds*
*1 cinnamon stick*
*1 teaspoon black peppercorns*
*1 bay leaf*

Cut the grapes from the main stem, leaving a small twig on each grape. Wash the grapes well in salted water. Drain them in a colander, then pack them into a sterilized jar. In a saucepan over medium heat, boil the vinegar and sugar until the sugar dissolves. Add the mustard seeds, cinnamon stick, black peppercorns, and bay leaf and return the mixture to a boil. Boil for 2 minutes, then pour the hot vinegar over the grapes. Cover and seal the jar. Store the grapes in a cool, dark place. Leave for 4 weeks before using.
MAKES 1 4-CUP JAR

# VERJUICE

*Verjuice, also called green juice, is the juice of under-ripe fruit, usually grapes and crab apples. It used to be cooked with goose, as a binder for the stuffing or to deglaze the pan for gravy, but was superseded by vinegar and lemon juice. Make verjuice in small amounts and keep it for cooking with fish and poultry. Traditionally the juice was extracted using a special press, but it can be made without one.*

INGREDIENTS
*2 pounds (1 kg) green grapes*

*RIGHT: Pickled Grapes with cheese and crusty bread makes a simple alfresco meal.*

De-stalk, wash, and dry the grapes. Place them in a metal chinois (thin mesh sieve) and press with the end of a wooden spoon or pestle to extract the juice. Strain the juice through a jelly bag without pressing to prevent clouding. Pour the juice into sterilized bottles and store them in a very cool cellar or in the refrigerator for 1 month before using.
MAKES ABOUT 2 CUPS.

# FIG AND ALMOND CONSERVE

*This conserve has whole figs in a thick syrup as well as almonds for added crunch.*

INGREDIENTS

3 cups (1½ pounds/750 g) white granulated sugar

¾ cup (185 mL) water

Zest of 1 lemon

3 pounds (1.5 kg) firm but ripe purple figs

1 lemon, thinly sliced

1 cup (5 ounces/155 g) blanched, toasted almond halves

½ cup (125 mL) cognac

Place the sugar, water, and lemon zest in a jam pan or a large, wide saucepan over low heat and cook for 5 minutes. Add the whole figs and lemon slices, bring to a boil, and simmer for 15 minutes. Remove the pan from the heat, cover with a dishcloth, and leave 12 hours or overnight. Return the pan to medium heat, bring the mixture to a boil, then simmer for 30 to 35 minutes or until the mixture is thick. Add the almonds and the cognac. Cook for a further 2 minutes. Remove the pan from the heat, and let stand for 10 minutes, stirring occasionally. Ladle the conserve into warmed, sterilized jars and seal. Wait 2 weeks before using.
MAKES ABOUT 4 TO 6 CUPS

# FIG AND RHUBARB JAM

*Sweet figs and astringent rhubarb marry well together in a flavorsome combination.*

INGREDIENTS

1 pound (500 g) fresh firm figs

6 pounds (3 kg) rhubarb

12 cups (6 pounds/3 kg) white granulated sugar

Juice of 2 lemons

Fine zest of 1 lemon

½ cup (2 ounces/60 g) cashew nuts

Cut the figs in half lengthwise and place them in a large bowl. Wash and chop the rhubarb stalks into ¾-inch (2 cm) lengths and add them to the bowl. Sprinkle on the sugar, cover and set aside overnight. The next day, place the contents of the bowl in a jam pan or a large, wide saucepan and add the lemon juice and the zest. Place the pan over high heat and bring the mixture to a boil. Continue boiling, stirring occasionally, until the jam thickens, about 1 to 1½ hours. Stir in the cashew nuts and cook, stirring, for a further 5 minutes. Remove the pan from the heat and let stand for 10 minutes. Stir the jam well and then ladle it into warmed, sterilized jars and seal.
MAKES ABOUT 6 CUPS

# FIGS IN BRANDY

*As far as I am concerned, the fig season is all too short. One of the easiest fig recipes to make is whole Figs in Brandy. Serve the figs chilled with cream or panna cotta (Italian cooked cream).*

INGREDIENTS

4½ cups (1½ pounds/750 g)
    moist brown sugar
2 cups (500 mL) water
6 cloves
2 cinnamon sticks
2 limes, sliced
16 large fresh figs
2 tablespoons preserved ginger,
    finely sliced
About 2 cups (500 mL) brandy

Place the sugar, water, cloves, cinnamon sticks, and lime slices in a large saucepan. Cook over low heat, stirring until the sugar dissolves. Add the figs and poach gently for 10 minutes. Remove the figs with a slotted spoon and layer them in sterilized jars with the lime slices, ginger slices, and cinnamon sticks. Continue to cook the remaining syrup until it is reduced a little, about 10 minutes. Add an equal quantity of brandy to syrup and fill the jars. Store the jars for 4 weeks before opening. Refrigerate after opening.

MAKES ABOUT 1 4-CUP JAR

---

FIGS

Figs, whether white, green, brown, or purple, are always delicious to eat and, when cut, they reveal their fragrant, seeded pink flesh. The entire fruit can be eaten, so there is no need to peel them. When buying figs, inspect them carefully for blemishes and press them lightly to check that they are not overripe. Figs are best eaten at room temperature to capture their full flavor.

Figs are better known as dried fruit in many parts of the world, owing to their extreme fragility.

---

# MELON AND PASSION FRUIT JAM

*Choose large, heavy passion fruits with wrinkled skin — these are the ripest ones.*

### INGREDIENTS

*2 pounds (1 kg) firm melon,*
  *any kind*
*4 cups (2 pounds/1 kg) white*
  *granulated sugar*
*Pulp of 20 passion fruits*
*Juice of 2 lemons*
*Zest of 1 lemon*

Peel and seed the melon and cut it into small dice. Place it in a bowl and sprinkle half the sugar over it. Cover and leave overnight. The next day, place the contents of the bowl in a jam pan or a large, wide saucepan and add the passion fruit pulp, lemon juice, and zest. Bring the mixture to a boil over high heat, stirring continuously. Warm the remaining sugar, add it to the pan, and continue to stir until the sugar dissolves. Boil rapidly until setting point is reached, about 30 minutes. Ladle the jam into warmed, sterilized jars and seal.
MAKES ABOUT 4 CUPS

# MELON MARMALADE

*This marmalade is really a cross between a jam and a marmalade.*

### INGREDIENTS

*2 pounds (1 kg) firm melon,*
  *any kind*
*3 large lemons*
*3 oranges*
*8 cups (2 liters) water*
*6 pounds (3 kg) white*
  *granulated sugar, warmed*

*RIGHT: I usually make Melon and Passion Fruit Jam with honeydew melon, which gives the jam the glowing golden color you see in the photograph.*

Peel, seed, and finely dice the melon. Thinly slice the lemons and oranges, reserving the seeds. Place the fruit in a bowl and pour the water over it. Tie the seeds in a muslin bag and add the bag to the bowl. Cover the bowl and leave overnight. The next day, empty the contents of the bowl into a jam pan or a large, wide saucepan and place the pan over high heat. Bring the mixture to a boil and cook until the fruit is tender, about 10 to 20 minutes. Remove the muslin bag, squeezing it to release the juice into the pan. Then add the warmed sugar, stirring until the sugar dissolves. Continue to boil until setting point is reached, about 45 minutes. Let the jam rest until a skin begins to form. Stir once, then ladle the marmalade into warmed, sterilized jars and seal.
MAKES ABOUT 10 CUPS

*RIGHT: Most melons blend successfully with other fruit flavors such as pineapple, citrus, passion fruit, and banana.*

# MELON AND PINEAPPLE JAM

*Honeydew, cantaloupe, and piemelon are the best melons to use in this jam.*

## INGREDIENTS

*6 pounds (3 kg) firm melon, peeled, seeded, cut into cubes*

*9 cups (4½ pounds/2.25 kg) white granulated sugar*

*1 firm, ripe pineapple, peeled, cored, and diced*

*Juice of 4 lemons*

*Zest of 2 lemons*

Place the melon in a nonreactive bowl and sprinkle 4 cups of the sugar over it. Cover and leave overnight. The next day, transfer the melon to a nonreactive pan. Add the pineapple to the pan with the remaining sugar, lemon juice, and zest. Bring the mixture to a boil, over medium heat, stirring occasionally. Reduce the heat and simmer until setting point is reached, about 40 to 50 minutes. Ladle the jam into warmed, sterilized jars and seal.

MAKES ABOUT 8 CUPS

# MELON JELLY

*Honeydew melon, cantaloupe, or piemelon can be used to make this jelly. The melon should be ripe but not mushy.*

INGREDIENTS
*8 pounds (4 kg) melon, any kind*
*8 cups (4 pounds/2 kg) white granulated sugar*
*6 lemons*
*Boiling water*
*Extra white granulated sugar*

Peel and seed the melon and cut it into thin slices. Place the melon slices in a large bowl and sprinkle the sugar over them. Cover with a dishcloth and leave overnight. Peel and slice the lemons and place them in another bowl. Just cover them with boiling water and leave them overnight.

The next day, place the contents of both bowls in a jam pan or a large, wide saucepan over high heat and bring the mixture to a boil. Boil until the fruit is very soft, about 15 to 20 minutes. Ladle the fruit into a jelly bag and allow it to drip into a bowl for 12 hours or overnight. Discard the fruit pulp left in the bag.

Measure the strained juice into the jam pan and for each cup (250 mL) juice add 1 cup (8 ounces/250 g) sugar. Place the pan over medium heat, stirring continuously. Bring the mixture to a boil and continue to boil until setting point is reached, about 25 to 30 minutes. Ladle the jelly into warmed, sterilized jars, allow to cool, and seal.

MAKES ABOUT 12 TO 15 CUPS

---

MELONS

Melon most likely originated in tropical Africa and many varieties have been bred in varying forms to suit climatic conditions from warm temperate through to tropical areas.

Melon belongs in the same *Cucurbitaceae* family as cucumber and squash. Melon flesh consists of 95 percent water with a remarkably low 5 percent sugar. Varieties such as winter melon, musk melon, cantaloupe, and watermelon can all be used for preserving as well as enjoyed raw for desserts and starters.

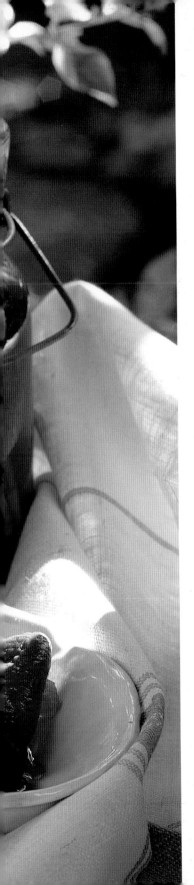

# Dried Fruit

*Autumn, the bringer of fruit, has poured out her riches,*

*and soon sluggish winter returns.*

HORACE

*LEFT: A jar of Winter Compote makes a wonderful gift to give to friends who don't like cooking but love eating.*

# BRANDIED FRUIT

*Brandied Fruit is very simple to make but it has many uses in a cook's kitchen.*

INGREDIENTS
*1 pound (500 g) good quality
   mixed dried fruit of choice*
*¼ cup (1 ounce/30 g) almonds*
*1 cinnamon stick*
*6 allspice berries*
*3 star anise*
*2 cloves*
*About 2 to 3 cups brandy*

Separate the small fruits, such as the raisins. Chop any larger fruits, such as apricots and pears, to the size of a raisin. Pack the fruits and almonds into a sterilized jar. Add the cinnamon stick, allspice berries, star anise, and cloves. Top up the jar with brandy and seal. Leave for 1 month in a cool, dark place before using. The dried fruit can be stored for 12 months if you can resist for that long.
MAKES ABOUT 4 CUPS

# WINTER COMPOTE

*Keep a large jar of winter compote ready to serve at any time with custard or cream.*

INGREDIENTS
*14 ounces (435 g) dried fruit of
   choice—prunes, figs, apples,
   pears, apricots, and dried
   chestnuts*
*4 cups (1 liter) lemon tea*
*Juice of 6 oranges*
*Juice and zest of 2 lemons*
*¼ cup (2 ounces/60 g) brown
   sugar*
*¼ cup (3 ounces/90 g) honey*
*2 cinnamon sticks*
*1 vanilla bean*
*⅓ cup (90 mL) brandy*

Place the dried fruit and the chestnuts in a saucepan and cover with the cooled tea. Bring the mixture to a boil over medium heat and cook for 5 minutes. Remove the saucepan from the heat and allow the fruit to cool. Drain and discard the tea. Place the fruit in a sterilized jar or container. Place the orange juice, lemon juice and zest, sugar, honey, cinnamon sticks, and vanilla bean in a saucepan over medium heat. Cook until the sugar and honey dissolve, stirring continuously, and bring the mixture to a boil. Remove the pan from the heat. When cooled, add the brandy and pour the brandy syrup over the fruit. Seal the jar. Store the compote in the refrigerator for up to 2 months.
MAKES 1 4-CUP JAR

*RIGHT: Serve Brandied Fruit with ice cream, puddings, custards, or homemade chocolates, or toss it into a fruit cake to make a quick Christmas cake.*

# MEDITERRANEAN SWEET AND SOUR FRUITS

*These fruits are a favorite in France and Italy. They are served with chargrilled duck or chicken breast or on an antipasto platter with salamis and prosciutto (Parma ham). I was given this recipe in Italy. It was a bit difficult to interpret, but worthwhile as the end result is so very good.*

INGREDIENTS

½ cup (3 ounces/90 g) dried figs

½ cup (3 ounces/90 g) dried seedless raisins

½ cup (3 ounces/90 g) dried pears

½ cup (3 ounces/90 g) dried apricots

1 small, fresh red chile (chilli)

1 clove garlic, peeled

2 fresh or dried bay leaves

1 cinnamon stick

3 cups (750 mL) red wine vinegar

1 tablespoon balsamic vinegar

3 tablespoons honey

Extra red wine vinegar

Separate the fruits and pack them into a large, sterilized jar. Add the chile, garlic, bay leaves, and cinnamon stick. Place the vinegars and the honey in a saucepan and heat over a medium heat, stirring to dissolve the honey. Pour the syrup over the fruit. Top up with extra red wine vinegar if required. Seal and store in a cool, dark place for 1 month before using the fruits. They will keep for 12 months.

MAKES ABOUT 2 TO 3 CUPS

---

RECONSTITUTING DRIED FRUIT

To reconstitute dried fruit, soak it in water, wine, spirits, or syrup for several hours. Add just enough liquid to cover it entirely, then add a little extra. If all the liquid is absorbed, add more a little at a time. If you are going to cook the fruit, cook it in the soaking water. Do not add sugar until the fruit has softened. Soak prunes in cold tea, while raisins, golden raisins (sultanas), and currants are best plumped up in boiling water for 10 minutes and then drained.

When buying dried fruit, choose clean fruit with no musty smell and store it in a cool, dry place. Though most of the vitamin C is lost in the drying process, vitamin A and many minerals are retained.

# DRIED FRUIT JAM

*This all-year-round jam makes a great gift. It's a very useful recipe because it doesn't rely on fruits in season.*

## INGREDIENTS

*4 ounces (125 g) dried apples*
*8 ounces (250 g) dried apricots*
*8 ounces (250 g) dried peaches*
*4 ounces (125 g) dried pears*
*4 ounces (125 g) dried figs*
*4 ounces (125 g) dried raisins*
*9 cups (2.25 liters) water*
*8 cups (4 pounds/2 kg) white granulated sugar, warmed*
*¾ cup (185 mL) fresh lemon juice*
*½ cup (125 mL) brandy*

Chop the fruits into small pieces (sharp kitchen scissors can make this job easier). Place the fruits in a large bowl and cover with the water. Set the bowl aside, covered with a dishcloth, for 24 hours.

Transfer the contents of the bowl to a jam pan or a large, wide saucepan and place over medium heat for 10 minutes. Add the warmed sugar and stir until it dissolves. Increase the heat and bring the mixture to a boil. Continue to boil rapidly for 20 minutes. Stir in the lemon juice. Continue to boil until setting point is reached, about 30 minutes. Remove the pan from the heat and stir in the brandy. Ladle the jam into warmed, sterilized jars and seal. Leave to mature for 4 weeks before opening.

MAKES ABOUT 8 CUPS

*RIGHT: The art of drying apricots has been perfected in California. The fruit is picked when just under-ripe, halved and pitted, placed in wooden trays, and stacked in sulfur houses which help to retain the color and flavor of the fruit. The trays are then placed in the sun to dry.*

# APRICOTS IN SHERRY

*One excellent way to serve Apricots in Sherry is to drain the apricots and dip them into melted dark chocolate. Serve them with coffee, or dice them for a piquant addition to ice creams and winter puddings.*

INGREDIENTS
*1 pound (500 g) soft dried*
*  apricots*
*Star anise*
*Allspice berries*
*3 cups (750 mL) sweet sherry*
*  or muscat*

Place the apricots in small, sterilized jars if you are making them for gifts; alternatively, use one large jar. To each jar add 1 to 2 star anise and a few allspice berries. Cover the fruit with sherry and seal. Store in a cool, dark place for up to 6 months. Leave the apricots to mature for 1 month before using them.

MAKES ABOUT 2 CUPS

# TIPSY PEARS

*Tipsy Pears are delicious served with mascarpone cheese. If you have time, drain and pat dry some pears, then dip half of each pear into melted dark chocolate.*

INGREDIENTS
*8 ounces (250 g) soft dried*
*  pears*
*Boiling water*
*Zest of 1 lemon*
*¾-inch (2 cm) knob fresh*
*  ginger, cut into thin strips*
*2 cloves*
*1 cinnamon stick*
*About 1 to 2 cups (250 to*
*  500 mL) Calvados*

Place the pears in a bowl and pour over just enough boiling water to cover them. Leave to stand for 10 minutes. Meanwhile, peel the lemon with a potato peeler and cut the zest into long, thin strips. Drain the pears well and pat dry with paper towels. Pack the pears into a sterilized jar, layering with the zest and the ginger strips. Add the cloves and cinnamon stick. Top up the jar with Calvados and seal. Store the jar in a cool, dark place for 12 months. The pears will be ready to use after 1 month.

MAKES ABOUT 2 CUPS

*RIGHT: I enjoy going to a bit of extra trouble to giftwrap preserves such as Apricots in Sherry, to give as Christmas and birthday presents.*

# MUSTARD FRUITS

*This unusual combination of fruits, mustard, and spices is a taste sensation.*

INGREDIENTS

¾ cup (185 mL) water

¾ cup (4 ounces/125 g) brown
  sugar

¼ cup (60 mL) lemon juice

⅓ cup (90 mL) wine vinegar

2 tablespoons Dijon mustard

1 clove garlic, crushed

10 whole cloves

2 cinnamon sticks

3 ounces (90 g) each of glacé
  figs, orange slices, and
  apricots

8 ounces (250 g) each of glacé
  pineapple and pears

Place the water, sugar, lemon juice, white wine vinegar, mustard, garlic, cloves, and cinnamon sticks in a saucepan over low heat and bring the mixture slowly to a boil. Add the fruits to the syrup and simmer for 10 minutes until the fruit is soft. Pack the fruit into a warmed, sterilized jar and strain the syrup over it. Cool and seal well. Store in the refrigerator until required. The fruits keep for 2 to 3 months stored in the refrigerator.

MAKES ABOUT 1 4-CUP JAR

# SPICED PRUNES

*When buying prunes, choose large soft ones with a deep blue-black color.*

INGREDIENTS

5 cups (2 pounds/1 kg) prunes

2½ cups (625 mL) red wine
  vinegar

Blade of mace

½ cinnamon stick

1 teaspoon black pepper

1 cup (5 ounces/155 g) brown
  sugar

10 whole blanched almonds

Allspice berries

About ½ cup (125 mL) brandy

Soak the prunes in water overnight. The next day, drain them well and pack them into sterilized jars. Place the vinegar, mace, cinnamon stick, pepper, and sugar in a saucepan and boil over medium heat for 5 minutes. Pour the reduced liquid over the prunes. Distribute the almonds between the jars and put 3 allspice berries into each jar along with 2 tablespoons brandy. Seal the jars tightly. Store the prunes in a cool, dry place. Keep the spiced prunes for 3 months before eating them.

MAKES ABOUT 6 CUPS

*RIGHT: Date Chutney makes a great snack when served with cheese, biscuits, and fruit. One of the oldest known cultivated fruits, the date has been grown in the Arab world, where it is a staple food, for over 7000 years. The best quality dates are sold whole and are preferable to those sold in compressed blocks.*

# DATE CHUTNEY

*Dates keep well, so they are generally available year-round.*

## INGREDIENTS

½ cup allspice berries

5½ cups (2 pounds/1 kg) pitted, soft, dried dates

1 pound (500 g) onions

2½ cups (625 mL) malt vinegar

6 tablespoons sea salt

1 teaspoon ground ginger

3 cups (1 pound/500 g) soft brown sugar

Tie the allspice berries in a muslin bag. Place the dates and chopped onions in a food processor and pulse until they are finely chopped but not mushy. Transfer the mixture to a nonreactive saucepan, add the remaining ingredients, bring to a boil and simmer over low heat until the chutney is thick, about 30 minutes. Remove the muslin bag. Allow the mixture to cool, then pour it into warmed, sterilized jars and seal.

MAKES ABOUT 6 CUPS

# DRUNKEN FIGS AND RAISINS

*In addition to terrific flavor, figs and raisins boast impressive amounts of fiber, iron, and potassium.*

INGREDIENTS
1½ *cups (8 ounces/250 g) soft*
  *dried figs*
2¼ *cups (12 ounces/375 g)*
  *seedless raisins*
¾-*inch (2 cm) knob of ginger*
10 *allspice berries*
1 *cinnamon stick*
1 *vanilla bean*
3 *cups (750 mL) brandy*

Pack the figs and raisins separately into sterilized jars, layering them with the ginger (cut into strips) and spices. Cover the fruits with brandy and seal the jars. Store in a cool, dark place for 12 months. They are ready to eat after 3 months, but they get better as they mature.

MAKES ABOUT 3 CUPS

# ALMOND PRUNE JAM

*The best prunes are from French d'Agen sugar plums.*

INGREDIENTS
5 *cups (2 pounds/1 kg) soft*
  *dried prunes*
1¼ *cups (310 mL) water*
1¼ *cups (300 mL) apple juice*
¾ *cup (3 ounces/90 g) blanched*
  *almonds, slivered*
1⅓ *cups (11 ounces/340 g) raw*
  *sugar, warmed*

*LEFT: Serve these delectable Drunken Figs and Raisins as a winter dessert with custard, mascarpone cheese, or ice cream.*

Halve and pit the prunes. Place the prunes in a bowl and cover them with the water and the juice. Cover the bowl with a dishcloth and leave to macerate overnight.

The next day, place the contents of the bowl into a jam pan or a large, wide saucepan. Add the almonds and bring the mixture to a boil over medium heat. Reduce to a simmer and add the warmed sugar. Stir until the sugar dissolves. Increase the heat to a constant bubble and cook until the jam reaches setting point, about 20 to 25 minutes. Ladle the jam into warmed, sterilized jars and seal.

MAKES ABOUT 6 CUPS

# Spicy Vegetables

The great galleys of Venice and Florence

Be well laden with things of complacence;

All spicerye and of grocers ware

With sweet wines, all manner of fare. . .

ADAM DE MOLYNEUX

*LEFT: A treasure-chest of homegrown vegetables: red and yellow bell peppers, red and yellow zucchini, red onions, tomatoes, eggplant, garlic, and chile.*

# ARTICHOKES IN OIL

*Small, fresh globe artichokes are the best ones to use.*

INGREDIENTS
*2 pounds (1 kg) artichokes*
*1 large lemon, halved*
*4 cups (1 liter) white wine*
  *vinegar*
*1 tablespoon sea salt*
*1 tablespoon dill seeds*
*1 tablespoon peppercorns*
*2 bay leaves*
*Sprigs fresh herbs, any variety*
*2 cloves garlic, peeled*
*2 small red chiles (chillies)*
*4 cups (1 liter) olive oil*

Remove the tough outer leaves and trim off the pointed tips of remaining leaves (scissors are easiest). Cut each artichoke in half lengthwise and rub the cut half with lemon to prevent browning. Place artichokes in a bowl of cold water with any remaining lemon juice. Leave for 1 hour. In a nonreactive saucepan, combine the vinegar, salt, dill seeds, peppercorns, and bay leaves and bring to a boil over medium heat. Drain the artichokes and add to boiling vinegar. Simmer for 10 minutes, then remove artichokes using a slotted spoon, drain, and dry on paper towels. Place the artichokes into warmed, sterilized wide-necked jars, layering with herbs, slices of garlic, and chiles. Cover with oil and seal. Store the artichokes in a cool, dark place for 4 weeks before using.
MAKES 6 CUPS

# GREEN BEAN CHUTNEY

*This chutney is a tasty accompaniment to meat or poultry.*

INGREDIENTS
*2 pounds (1 kg) green beans,*
  *trimmed, and cut into ¾-inch*
  *(2 cm) lengths*
*3 cups (750 mL) wine vinegar*
*¼ cup (1 ounce/30 g) raisins*
*1 teaspoon grainy mustard*
*1½ tablespoons cornstarch*
*1¼ pounds (625 g) onions*
*4 cups (1¼ pounds/625 g)*
  *brown sugar*
*1 tablespoon ground turmeric*

Place the beans and ⅔ cup (170 mL) of the wine vinegar in a large, nonreactive saucepan over medium heat. Bring the vinegar to a boil and cook the beans for 15 minutes. Add the remaining ingredients (peeling and chopping the onions) and return to a boil. Cook for 10 minutes, stirring continuously, until the chutney has thickened. Ladle it into sterilized jars, allow to cool, and then seal. Store the chutney for 3 weeks before opening. It will keep well for 4 to 6 months.
MAKES ABOUT 6 CUPS

*RIGHT: When making Artichokes in Oil, seek out small to medium artichokes and avoid large, woody ones.*

# PICKLED ASPARAGUS

*This pickle is best made in small batches as it keeps for only 6 weeks.*

### INGREDIENTS

*2 bunches fresh asparagus
  (about 20 stalks), trimmed*
*2½ cups (625 mL) white wine
  vinegar*
*10 white peppercorns*
*1 bay leaf*
*½ teaspoon freshly grated
  nutmeg*

Wash the asparagus in cold water and leave it to soak in salted water for 4 hours. Place the vinegar, peppercorns, bay leaf, and nutmeg in a saucepan. Boil over medium heat for 5 minutes. Remove the saucepan from the heat and allow the mixture to cool. Blanch the asparagus in boiling water for 1 minute, then place on a clean dishcloth to cool. Pack the asparagus into a tall jar, standing the spears upright. Cover with the cold vinegar and seal. It is ready to eat after 2 weeks.

MAKES 6 CUPS

# PICKLED BABY CARROTS

*Tangy pickled carrots are delicious as well as nutritious.*

### INGREDIENTS

*2 bunches baby carrots*
*4 to 5 cups (1 to 1.25 liters)
  white wine vinegar*
*2 cups (1 pound/500 g) white
  granulated sugar*
*1 teaspoon celery seeds*
*1 teaspoon white peppercorns*
*1 teaspoon dill seeds*
*1 teaspoon mustard seeds*
*1 bay leaf*
*Extra bay leaves for decoration*

Cut the carrots from the bunches, leaving short stalks. There is no need to peel baby carrots. Place the vinegar, sugar, spices, and bay leaf in a nonreactive pan and bring the mixture to a boil, stirring constantly, over medium heat. Add the carrots and cook for 1 minute, or longer if you prefer them softer. Remove the pan from the heat. Lift out the carrots with a slotted spoon and pack them into warmed, sterilized jars. Discard the bay leaf. Pour in hot vinegar to cover the carrots, insert a bay leaf down the side of each jar, and seal. Store the carrots in a cool, dark place for up to 3 months. Leave the carrots for 2 weeks before eating them.

MAKES ABOUT 4 CUPS

*RIGHT: Pickled Asparagus can be made with green, white, and purple asparagus.*

# RED BELL PEPPER JELLY

*Choose firm, thick-skinned bell peppers (capsicums), with shiny skins and no blemishes.*

INGREDIENTS
*2 pounds (1 kg) firm red bell
  peppers (capsicums)
2 cups (500 mL) white wine
  vinegar
2 teaspoons sea salt
2 small red chiles (chillies)
10 cups (5 pounds/2.5 kg)
  white granulated sugar
Juice of 2 lemons
6 teaspoons powdered citrus
  pectin*

Halve and seed the bell peppers. Cut them into small pieces and finely chop them in a food processor or blender. Place in a nonreactive pan and add the remaining ingredients (seeding and chopping the chiles), except for the powdered pectin. Put the pan over medium heat and bring the mixture to a boil, stirring. Reduce the heat to a simmer and cook for about 1 hour. Add the powdered pectin, increase the heat, and boil for 2 minutes, stirring constantly. Skim the surface to remove any scum. Remove the pan from the heat, ladle the jelly into warmed, sterilized jars, and seal. It will be ready to eat after 2 weeks.

MAKES ABOUT 10 CUPS

# RED BELL PEPPERS PRESERVED IN OIL

*Preserved red peppers add vibrant color and flavor to any dish.*

INGREDIENTS
*4 pounds (2 kg) firm red bell
  peppers (capsicums)
A few black peppercorns
4 cloves garlic, peeled
2 bay leaves
2 fresh, small red chiles
  (chillies)
8 cups (2 liters) olive oil*

Grill the bell peppers under the broiler (griller) or hold them on a long skewer over a gas flame. While they're still hot, place them in a plastic bag to sweat a little, then peel off the charred skin. Remove the stalks and seeds and cut the flesh into strips. Pack the pepper strips into sterilized jars, adding the peppercorns, garlic, bay leaves, and chiles, and add olive oil to cover. Insert a skewer down the side of each jar to expel any air bubbles. Seal and store in the refrigerator for up to 3 months. The bell peppers can be eaten immediately.

MAKES 2 4-CUP JARS

*LEFT: Red Bell Pepper Jelly
glowing in the afternoon light.*

# CORN AND CABBAGE RELISH

*This colorful relish has lots of flavor and crunch.*

INGREDIENTS

1 pound (500 g) fresh corn cobs
3 ounces (90 g) cabbage
2 red bell peppers (capsicums)
2 sticks celery, sliced thinly
⅓ cup (3 ounces/90 g) white
   granulated sugar
2 tablespoons mustard seeds
2 teaspoons sea salt
1 teaspoon celery seeds
2½ cups (625 mL) white wine
   vinegar

Cut the corn kernels from the cobs. Chop the cabbage and seed and dice the bell peppers. Place the corn kernels, cabbage, bell peppers, and celery in a large, nonreactive pan and just cover with water. Bring the water to a boil over medium heat and cook the vegetables for 1 minute, then drain. Return the vegetables to the pan and add the remaining ingredients. Bring the mixture to a boil over medium heat and cook for 5 minutes. Ladle the relish into warmed, sterilized jars, allow to cool, and then seal. This relish is best stored in the refrigerator. Bring it to room temperature before serving.

MAKES ABOUT 4 CUPS

# CORN RELISH

*Spices enliven the farm-fresh taste of sweet corn.*

INGREDIENTS

12 fresh corn cobs
1 red bell pepper (capsicum)
1 small green bell pepper
   (capsicum)
2 teaspoons sea salt
2 teaspoons mustard seeds
1 teaspoon dry mustard
½ teaspoon ground turmeric
1½ cups (375 mL) cider vinegar
1 cup (8 ounces/250 g) white
   granulated sugar

Remove the corn kernels from the cobs, seed and finely chop the bell peppers, and then place all the ingredients in a nonreactive pan. Bring the mixture to a boil over high heat and then reduce the heat and simmer for 30 minutes. Ladle the relish into sterilized jars, cool, and seal. Store the relish in a cool, dark place.

MAKES ABOUT 3 CUPS

# BRINJAL CHUTNEY

*This sweet and spicy eggplant chutney is an excellent accompaniment to curries and cold meats. It improves with age so it is best to leave a jar for a month or two before opening to allow the harshness of the vinegar to mellow.*

INGREDIENTS

*4 pounds (2 kg) eggplants (aubergines)*

*2 tablespoons sea salt*

*3 onions, chopped*

*2 red bell peppers (capsicums), seeded and chopped*

*½ cup (3 ounces/90 g) raisins*

*2 fresh, small, red chiles (chillies), seeded and chopped*

*4 cloves garlic, chopped*

*1 teaspoon ground ginger*

*1 teaspoon ground allspice*

*2 cups (10 ounces/310 g) brown sugar*

*3½ cups (875 mL) white wine vinegar*

Cut the stalk ends off the eggplants and cut the eggplants into small dice. Place in a colander, sprinkle with the salt, and cover with a dishcloth. Set aside for 4 hours. Rinse the eggplant and pat dry. Place the eggplant and the remaining ingredients in a large, nonreactive pan over medium heat and stir until the sugar dissolves. Bring to a boil and simmer until the chutney thickens, about 40 minutes. Ladle into warmed, sterilized jars, allow to cool, and then seal. The chutney is ready to eat after 1 month.

MAKES ABOUT 6 TO 8 CUPS

---

EGGPLANT

Buy eggplants with firm, smooth, glossy, unblemished skins and green stems. Avoid very large, soft ones.

Eggplants rarely need to be disgorged, that is, sprinkled with salt to extract any bitter juices. It is only necessary if they are large ones and not very fresh. Test for bitterness by cooking a piece. The small varieties do not ever need to be disgorged.

# BEET CHUTNEY

*This sweet root vegetable makes a colorful red chutney.*

INGREDIENTS

2 pounds (1 kg) fresh beets
  (beetroots)
1 pound (500 g) cooking apples
1 large onion, peeled and
  chopped
1 tablespoon finely chopped
  fresh ginger
1 level teaspoon sea salt
1 cup (5 ounces/155 g) brown
  sugar
1¼ cups (310 mL) cider vinegar

Trim the beets, leaving short stalks. Place them in a saucepan, just cover with water, and bring the water to a boil over medium heat. Cover the pan, reduce the heat, and simmer for 40 to 50 minutes or until the beets are tender when tested with a skewer. Drain, cool, and remove the skins. Dice and set aside. Peel, core, and chop the apples. Place the apples in a large, nonreactive pan and add the remaining ingredients. Stir over medium heat until the sugar dissolves. Bring to a boil and simmer until the apple is tender, about 45 minutes. Ladle the chutney into warmed, sterilized jars, cover until cool, and then seal.
MAKES ABOUT 4 TO 5 CUPS

# PICKLED BABY BEETS

*Baby beets (beetroots) can be served whole. Slice or quarter the larger ones.*

INGREDIENTS

4 pounds (2 kg) baby beets
  (beetroots)

Spiced vinegar
4 cups (1 liter) cider vinegar
1 cinnamon stick
1 teaspoon ground mace
1 teaspoon ground allspice
1 teaspoon ground cloves
8 black peppercorns

*RIGHT: Beet Chutney is excellent eaten with salads and cold ham.*

Trim the beets carefully, leaving a little of the stalks on and taking care not to pierce the skins or the beets will bleed. Place the beets in a saucepan and just cover them with water. Bring the water to a boil and cook over medium heat until they are tender when pricked with a skewer, about 5 to 10 minutes. Remove the skins when cool.

To make the spiced vinegar, place the vinegar and the spices in a saucepan over medium heat, bring the vinegar to a boil, and boil for 5 minutes. Remove the saucepan from the heat and leave it aside to cool. Pack the beets into sterilized jars, cover them with the spiced vinegar, and seal. Store the beets in a cool, dark place for 4 months. They will be ready to eat after 2 weeks.
MAKES ABOUT 2 4-CUP JARS

# PICKLED RED CABBAGE

*Vibrant red cabbage makes a simple and hearty pickle.*

INGREDIENTS

*4 pounds (2 kg) red cabbage*

*4 tablespoons sea salt*

*4 cups (1 liter) white vinegar*

*1 teaspoon each mustard seeds
  and peppercorns*

*1 bay leaf*

Remove and discard the outer leaves of each cabbage. Cut each cabbage in half and cut out the coarse white core. Shred each half finely. Separate the shreds in a large bowl and sprinkle on the salt. Cover with a dishcloth and let stand overnight. The next day, drain the cabbage, rinse it in cold water, and drain again. Pack the cabbage into sterilized jars. Bring the vinegar and spices to a boil, then cool. Add the cold spiced vinegar to the jars and seal. Store the cabbage in a cool, dark place for up to 12 months. Leave for 2 to 3 weeks before using.

MAKES ABOUT 8 CUPS

# CUCUMBER PICKLES

*Classic pickles, made at home, have a taste unlike any commercial variety.*

INGREDIENTS

*3 pounds (1.5 kg) cucumbers
  (Lebanese, telegraph, or any
  long, thin variety)*

*1 pound (500 g) onions*

*1 green bell pepper (capsicum)*

*1 red bell pepper (capsicum)*

*2 tablespoons sea salt*

*2 cups (10 ounces/310 g)
  brown sugar*

*2 teaspoons mustard seeds*

*2 teaspoons celery seeds*

*1 teaspoon turmeric*

*4 cups (1 liter) white wine
  vinegar*

Slice the cucumbers into ⅛-inch (2 mm) slices. Peel and slice the onions thinly, and seed and cut the bell peppers into thin strips. Layer the vegetables into a colander, sprinkling each layer with salt. Cover with a dishcloth and leave to stand for 3 hours. Drain, rinse well, and drain again. Place the sugar, spices, and vinegar in a nonreactive pan and bring it to a boil over medium heat. Add the drained vegetables, return to boiling point, stirring, then turn off the heat immediately. Pack the vegetables into sterilized jars, then add the spiced vinegar. Cool and seal. Store the pickles in a cool, dark place.

MAKES ABOUT 5 TO 6 CUPS

*RIGHT: Pickled Red Cabbage can be served cold or hot to accompany roast duck, lamb, or pork.*

# PICKLED MUSHROOMS

*You can buy prepared pickling spice in small packets from your supermarket or delicatessen.*

INGREDIENTS

*4 cups (1 liter) white wine
    vinegar
2 tablespoons pickling spice
3 teaspoons sea salt
6 cloves garlic, peeled
3 bay leaves
Sprigs of oregano
Black peppercorns
2 fresh red chiles (chillies)
2 pounds (1 kg) button
    mushrooms*

Place all the ingredients except the mushrooms in a large, nonreactive saucepan over medium heat. Bring the mixture to a boil and add the mushrooms. Turn off the heat and leave the mushrooms in the liquid for 5 minutes. Remove them with a slotted spoon and pack them into sterilized jars. Add enough pickling vinegar to completely cover the mushrooms. Seal and leave for 4 weeks. Once a jar is opened, store it in the refrigerator.

MAKES ABOUT 2 4-CUP JARS

# SQUASH CHUTNEY

*Soft summer squash makes a rich and flavorful chutney.*

INGREDIENTS

*6 pounds (3 kg) squash
    (marrow)
2 tablespoons sea salt
2 large cooking apples
1½ onions
½ cup (3 ounces/90 g) raisins
½ cup (3 ounces/90 g) golden
    raisins (sultanas)
1¼ cups (6 ounces/185 g)
    brown sugar
1 teaspoon ground ginger
2 teaspoons mustard seeds
4 cups (1 liter) cider vinegar*

Peel the squash, remove the seeds, and cut the flesh into small cubes. Place it in a bowl and sprinkle on the salt. Cover the bowl with a dishcloth and leave overnight. The next day, drain and rinse the squash, place it in a nonreactive pan, and add the remaining ingredients. Bring the mixture to a boil over medium heat and simmer until it is thick, stirring occasionally, for about 1½ hours. Ladle the chutney into warmed, sterilized jars, allow to cool, and then seal. The chutney will be ready to eat after 1 month.

MAKES ABOUT 6 CUPS

*LEFT: These Pickled Mushrooms have been prepared from cultivated mushrooms, but if can gather wild cèpes and morels, they would be even more delicious.*

# RED ONION CHUTNEY

*The freshest onions are those that are firm, shiny, and mild-smelling.*

### INGREDIENTS
¼ cup (60 mL) olive oil

3 pounds (1.5 kg) red onions

1 green apple, grated

1½ cups (375 mL) red wine
vinegar

12 soft prunes, pitted

1½ cups (12 ounces/375 g) raw
(demerara) sugar

1 teaspoon sea salt

½ teaspoon white pepper

½ teaspoon ground allspice

Heat the oil in a large, nonreactive pan. Peel and thinly slice the onions and add them to the pan. Cook over low heat, stirring occasionally, for 1 hour. Add the remaining ingredients and stir until the sugar dissolves. Simmer until the chutney has thickened, about 1 hour (note that it will be more liquid than most chutneys, but will thicken further as it cools). Ladle into sterilized jars, leave to cool, then seal. Leave the chutney for 3 to 4 weeks before using.
MAKES ABOUT 4 TO 5 CUPS

# TURNIP CHUTNEY

*Turnips have a mild flavor that pairs well with many dishes.*

### INGREDIENTS
2 pounds (1 kg) turnips

1 pound (500 g) cooking apples

1 pound (500 g) onions

½ teaspoon ground turmeric

6 cups (1.5 liters) white wine
vinegar

2 teaspoons mustard seeds

¾ cup (4 ounces/125 g) golden
raisins (sultanas)

½ cup (3 ounces/90 g) brown
sugar

1 teaspoon ground coriander

1 teaspoon sea salt

¼ teaspoon white pepper

Wash and peel the turnips, slice them thickly, and cook in boiling water until soft, about 15 minutes. Drain and mash. Peel, core, and dice the apples and chop the onions. Place all the ingredients in a large, nonreactive pan over medium heat. Stir for 5 minutes, bring the mixture to a boil, then simmer until the chutney is thick, about 50 to 60 minutes. Ladle the chutney into warmed, sterilized jars, allow to cool, and then seal.
MAKES ABOUT 5 TO 6 CUPS

*RIGHT: Red Onion Chutney is very tasty served with cold meats, terrines, and pâtés.*

# PUMPKIN AND ROSEMARY JAM

*Hard pumpkin or winter squash is best for this jam.*

INGREDIENTS
*6 pounds (3 kg) pumpkin*
*3 cups (1½ pounds/750 g) white granulated sugar, warmed*
*3 sprigs of rosemary*
*Juice of 2 lemons*
*Zest of 1 lemon*

*ABOVE: A hard pumpkin, known in Australia as Queensland Blue.*

Peel, seed, and dice the pumpkin. Place it in a jam pan or a large, wide saucepan with enough cold water to just cover the pumpkin. Bring the water to a boil and cook over medium heat until the pumpkin is soft. Add the warmed sugar and stir until it dissolves. Place the rosemary sprigs in a muslin bag and add it to the pan. Add the lemon juice and zest. Simmer for 1 hour. Lift out the muslin bag, squeeze it over the pan, and discard. Ladle the jam into warmed, sterilized jars and seal.
MAKES ABOUT 6 CUPS

# PUMPKIN CHUTNEY

*When I was growing up in the country, my father grew an abundance of Queensland Blue pumpkins. These sat for months maturing on the hot tin roof of the outside toilet, waiting for my mother to make into delicious dishes like this chutney.*

INGREDIENTS

2 pounds (1 kg) firm, ripe
   pumpkin or winter squash
4 firm tomatoes
4 green cooking apples
2 onions
2 cloves garlic, finely chopped
¾ cup (4 ounces/125 g) raisins
2 cups (10 ounces/310 g)
   brown sugar
1 tablespoon sea salt
1 teaspoon ground cloves
1 tablespoon chopped fresh
   rosemary needles
1 teaspoon freshly ground black
   pepper
3 to 3½ cups (750 to 875 mL)
   cider vinegar

Peel and chop the pumpkin into small dice, about ⅜ inch (1 cm) across. Peel and roughly chop the tomatoes, apples, and onions. Place all the ingredients in a large, nonreactive saucepan over low heat and bring the mixture to a boil. Maintain the heat so the chutney bubbles slowly and cook for 1 hour or until the chutney thickens. Squash will not take quite as long as pumpkin. Ladle the chutney into warmed, sterilized jars, allow to cool, and then seal. The jars can be opened after 4 weeks.

MAKES ABOUT 8 TO 10 CUPS

PUMPKINS

Pumpkins vary in their skin color, size, and shape — from large round, dark green skin, to elongated, yellow and orange skin — but the flesh inside is always that same wonderful, warm orange color. Pumpkins are a favorite savory vegetable, enjoyed roasted, puréed into soup, or as a pie filling. This versatile food also makes aromatic chutneys and jams. Pumpkin stores well, which makes it invaluable as a basic pantry ingredient.

# PICKLED SHALLOTS

*The shallots should be kept in a cool, dark, dry place for 4 to 6 weeks before opening.*

### INGREDIENTS

*4 pounds (2 kg) golden shallots*
*1 cup (8 ounces/250 g) sea salt*
*5 cups (1.25 liters) spiced vinegar (page 112)*
*2 tablespoons mustard seeds*
*10 black peppercorns*
*⅓ cup (3 ounces/90 g) white granulated sugar*
*4 to 6 fresh, small, red chiles (chillies)*
*Bay leaves*

Place the shallots in a large bowl and cover with water and ⅓ cup (3 ounces/90 g) of the salt. Leave overnight, covered. Drain off the water and peel the shallots. Dissolve the remaining salt in 7 cups (1.75 liters) water in a large bowl and add the shallots. Place a plate on top of the bowl to keep the shallots submerged. Leave them for 24 hours, then drain. Pour the vinegar into a large, nonreactive pan and add the mustard seeds, black peppercorns, and sugar. Boil over medium heat, stirring continuously. Lower the heat and simmer for 5 minutes. Skim off any surface scum. Pack the shallots into sterilized jars and place 2 or 3 chiles and a bay leaf in each jar. Pour in the hot vinegar to cover. The shallots will keep for up to 6 months.
MAKES ABOUT 2 4-CUP JARS

# ZUCCHINI RELISH

*This relish is ready to eat in 2 weeks and keeps for 6 months.*

### INGREDIENTS

*5 pounds (2.5 kg) zucchini*
*8 onions*
*½ cup (4 ounces/125 g) sea salt*
*2 red bell peppers (capsicums)*
*2 cups (500 mL) white wine vinegar*
*1 cup ( 8 ounces/250 g) sugar*
*1 teaspoon each of mustard seeds, dry mustard, celery seeds, and ground allspice*
*½ teaspoon ground black pepper*

Chop the zucchini and onions, place them in a large bowl, and sprinkle with the salt. Cover with a dishcloth and set aside in a cool place overnight. The next day, drain the vegetables, rinse them in cold water, and drain again. Seed and chop the bell peppers, then place all the ingredients in a large, nonreactive pan over high heat and stir until the mixture comes to a boil. Reduce the heat and simmer, uncovered, for 30 to 50 minutes or until the relish is thick. Ladle the relish into warmed, sterilized jars, cool, and seal.
MAKES ABOUT 6 CUPS

*RIGHT: The delicate flavor of Pickled Shallots makes a pleasant change from pickled onions.*

# Tomatoes

*Without rising from my chair I could pick a ripe tomato from the vine, sprinkle salt on the warm spot which an instant before had been gilded by the sun, and bite deep into its juicy, full-flavoured succulence. As some other writer has said in some other context, I shall not look upon its like again.*

WAVERLEY ROOT

LEFT: *A member of the nightshade family, the tomato was once thought to be poisonous. Today, this 'fruit' is one of our most popular 'vegetables'.*

# DRIED TOMATOES

*Make sure the oven is not too warm or the tomatoes will cook rather than dry.*

INGREDIENTS

*2 pounds (1 kg) ripe Roma
(plum) tomatoes, halved
4 tablespoons sea salt
Freshly ground black pepper
1 tablespoon dried marjoram
1 tablespoon dried basil
Bay leaves
Black peppercorns
2 cloves garlic, cut into slivers
Extra virgin olive oil*

Scoop out the tomato seeds with your fingers, and discard, leaving the fibrous tissue intact. Place the halves, cut side up, on a baking sheet lined with parchment paper. Sprinkle with the salt, pepper, marjoram, and basil. Place the tray in a preheated oven at 210°F (100°C) for 12 hours. If the tomatoes are drying out too quickly, leave the oven door slightly ajar. When the tomatoes are dry and have cooled, pack them into a sterilized jar. Add a bay leaf, a few peppercorns, and some garlic slivers, cover with olive oil, and seal. Store in a cool, dry, dark place for up to 3 months. Refrigerate once the jar is opened.

MAKES 1 4-CUP JAR

# TOMATO WALNUT JAM

*Chopped walnuts add a rich flavor to this simple tomato jam.*

INGREDIENTS

*2 pounds (1 kg) firm ripe
tomatoes, sliced
4 cups (2 pounds/1 kg) white
granulated sugar
Juice of 2 lemons
Zest of 1 lemon
½ cup (2 ounces/60 g) chopped
walnuts*

Place the tomatoes in a large bowl, and cover with the sugar. Place a dishcloth over the bowl and leave to stand overnight. The next day, transfer the contents of the bowl to a jam pan or a large, wide saucepan and bring the mixture to a boil. Add the lemon juice and the zest. Reduce the heat slightly to a slow boil and cook until the jam reaches setting point, about 30 minutes. Stir in the walnuts and cook for 2 minutes. Remove the jam from the heat and let stand for another 10 minutes. Stir well again and then ladle the jam into warmed, sterilized jars and seal. The jam can be eaten after 1 month and should be stored in the refrigerator once a jar is opened.

MAKES ABOUT 4 TO 6 CUPS

*RIGHT: Oven-dried Tomatoes
develop a very special, deep
tomato flavor.*

# TOMATO KETCHUP

*The best cooking tomatoes are large, fully ripe beefsteak or round tomatoes.*

### INGREDIENTS
*8 pounds (4 kg) ripe tomatoes*
*4 onions*
*6 cloves garlic*
*10 each of allspice berries,*
  *peppercorns, and cloves*
*1 bay leaf*
*5 cups (1.25 liters) white wine*
  *vinegar*
*1½ cups (12 ounces/375 g)*
  *white granulated sugar*
*2 tablespoons mustard powder*
*2 teaspoons sea salt*

Roughly chop the tomatoes, onions, and garlic and place them in a large, nonreactive pan. Place the allspice berries, peppercorns, cloves, and bay leaf in a muslin bag, tie it up, and add it to the pan. Cook slowly over low heat until the vegetables are soft, stirring occasionally. Remove and discard the muslin bag. Spoon the vegetables into a blender or food processor and blend to a purée. Return the pulp to the pan and add the vinegar, sugar, mustard powder, and salt. Bring the mixture to a boil over medium heat and cook for about 1 hour, stirring occasionally. If the mixture is too thick, add a little more vinegar. When cooled, pour the ketchup into sterilized bottles and seal. It is ready to eat after 2 weeks.
MAKES ABOUT 6 CUPS

# TOMATO CHUTNEY

*Choose firm, ripe summer and fall tomatoes at their peak of flavor.*

### INGREDIENTS
*2 pounds (1 kg) tomatoes*
*1 pound (500 g) onions*
*1 cup (5 ounces/155 g) pitted*
  *dates*
*1 teaspoon sea salt*
*1½ cups (8 ounces/250 g)*
  *brown sugar*
*2 cups (500 mL) malt vinegar*
*2-inch (5 cm) piece ginger*
*1 teaspoon mustard seeds*
*½ teaspoon ground cloves*
*½ teaspoon ground black pepper*

Chop the tomatoes, peel and chop the onions, and roughly chop the dates. Place in a nonreactive pan and add the remaining ingredients. Bring the mixture to a boil over medium heat, stirring constantly. Reduce the heat and simmer until the chutney has thickened, about 40 to 50 minutes. Ladle the chutney into warmed, sterilized jars, allow to cool, and then seal. The chutney is ready to use after 1 month.
MAKES ABOUT 5 CUPS

# CURRIED TOMATO CHUTNEY

*Use firm, ripe tomatoes for making pickles and chutneys.*

## INGREDIENTS

6 pounds (3 kg) tomatoes
Boiling water
3 large onions
6 cloves garlic
2-inch (5 cm) piece fresh ginger
1 cup (5 ounces/155 g) brown
  sugar
1 tablespoon curry powder
1 teaspoon cayenne pepper
2 teaspoons sea salt
1 cup (6 ounces/185 g) soft
  golden raisins (sultanas)
1 teaspoon mustard seeds
2 teaspoons coriander seeds
1¼ cups (310 mL) white wine
  vinegar

To peel the tomatoes, cut a cross in the base of each tomato, place them in a bowl, and cover with boiling water for 1 minute to loosen the skins. Drain, remove the skins, and dice the flesh. Place the tomato dice in a large, nonreactive pan. Peel and chop the onions, garlic, and ginger, place them in the pan, and add the remaining ingredients. Bring the mixture to a boil over medium heat, stirring constantly. Reduce the heat and simmer until the chutney has thickened, about 1 hour. It may take longer if the tomatoes are watery. Ladle the chutney into warmed, sterilized jars and seal. Leave for 2 months before opening.

MAKES ABOUT 10 CUPS

---

### TOMATOES

When buying tomatoes make sure the skins are smooth, shiny, and unblemished. Tomatoes should weigh heavily in the hand and they are best when firm. Keep them out of the refrigerator as chilling dulls the flavor.

Selective breeding of the tomato plant has produced differences in size, shape, color, productivity, and hardiness. Unfortunately some of these attributes have come to be regarded as more important than the flavor! It has only been in recent years that some growers have started to concentrate on bringing back the flavor. The cherry tomato generally has the true tomato flavor.

# GREEN TOMATO AND ONION CHUTNEY

*I developed this recipe to make good use of an oversupply of homegrown tomatoes. The chutney never lasts long in my house.*

INGREDIENTS

*2 pounds (1 kg) green tomatoes*
*1 pound (500 g) onions*
*1 pound (500 g) cooking apples*
*2¼ cups (575 mL) wine vinegar*
*1½ cups (8 ounces/250 g)*
  *golden raisins (sultanas)*
*½ teaspoon sea salt*
*½ teaspoon cayenne pepper*
*1 tablespoon chopped ginger*
*2 cloves garlic, finely chopped*

Chop the tomatoes, peel and chop the onions, and peel, core, and chop the apples. Place them in a nonreactive pan and add half the wine vinegar. Bring the mixture to a boil and cook, stirring, over medium heat for 45 minutes. Add the remaining vinegar and the other ingredients and simmer over medium heat, stirring occasionally, until the chutney thickens, about 20 to 30 minutes. Ladle the chutney into warmed, sterilized jars. Cover with a cloth and seal when cold. It will keep for up to 12 months.
MAKES 2 TO 3 CUPS

# GREEN TOMATO RELISH

*For a spicy relish, add cayenne pepper and ½ teaspoon each of ground ginger and cloves.*

INGREDIENTS

*5 pounds (2.5 kg) green*
  *tomatoes*
*1 pound (500 g) cooking apples*
*2 onions*
*2 garlic cloves*
*4½ cups (1½ pounds/750 g)*
  *brown sugar*
*2½ cups white wine vinegar*
*1 tablespoon sea salt*
*1 cup (5 ounces/155 g) golden*
  *raisins (sultanas)*
*1 teaspoon ground cinnamon*

Chop the tomatoes and peel, core, and dice the apples. Peel and chop the onions and garlic. Place them in a nonreactive pan and add the remaining ingredients. Bring the mixture to a boil, stirring occasionally. Reduce the heat and simmer until the chutney thickens, about 1 hour. Ladle it into warmed, sterilized jars, allow to cool, and then seal. The relish will be ready to eat after 1 month and should be refrigerated after opening.
MAKES ABOUT 6 CUPS

*LEFT: Green Tomato and Onion Chutney goes well with cheese and any cold meats. I also like to eat it on crusty bread topped with a few fresh tomato slices. A perfect working-day lunch.*

*RIGHT: Fresh locally grown chiles (chillies)—jalapeño, red, and yellow chiles.*

# CHILE TOMATO CHUTNEY

*Hot chiles marry with sweet tomatoes and tart apples to produce a unique flavor.*

INGREDIENTS

*3 pounds (1.5 kg) tomatoes*

*3 ounces (90 kg) golden shallots*

*14 ounces (435 g) cooking apples*

*3 fresh red chiles (chillies)*

*1¼ cups (6 ounces/185 g) hazelnuts*

*1 cup (6 ounces/185 g) golden raisins (sultanas)*

*¾ cup (6 ounces/185g) raw (demerara) sugar*

*2 teaspoons sea salt*

*1 teaspoon cayenne pepper*

*1 tablespoon mustard seeds*

*1 teaspoon ground ginger*

*1¼ cups (310 mL) white wine vinegar*

Chop the tomatoes, finely chop the shallots, peel and chop the apples, seed and chop the chiles, and roughly chop the hazelnuts. Place all the ingredients in a large, nonreactive saucepan over medium heat. Bring the mixture to a boil, reduce the heat to a simmer, and cook, stirring occasionally, until the ingredients are soft and the chutney thickens, about 30 to 50 minutes. Ladle the chutney into warmed, sterilized jars, allow to cool, and then seal. Store the chutney for 4 to 6 weeks before eating it.

MAKES ABOUT 8 CUPS

# RED TOMATO AND FRUIT RELISH

*This tasty relish requires some preparation time but it is worth the effort for barbecues, cold platters, and sandwiches.*

INGREDIENTS

1 cup (250 mL) white wine
  vinegar
2 cups (10 ounces/310 g)
  brown sugar
2 cloves garlic, finely chopped
2-inch (5 cm) piece fresh ginger,
  finely chopped
2 teaspoons curry powder
½ teaspoon ground cloves
½ teaspoon ground cinnamon
1 teaspoon freshly ground black
  pepper
1 teaspoon mustard seeds
1 teaspoon celery seeds
2 teaspoons sea salt
4 pounds (2 kg) firm tomatoes,
  peeled and chopped
1 pound (500 g) cooking
  apples, peeled, cored, and
  chopped
8 ounces (250 g) dried figs,
  chopped
8 ounces (250 g) dried pears,
  chopped
¾ cup (4 ounces/125 g) golden
  raisins (sultanas)
¾ cup (4 ounces/125 g) raisins
Juice and zest of 1 lemon

Place the vinegar and the sugar in a large, nonreactive pan over medium heat and stir until the sugar dissolves. Add the garlic, ginger, curry powder, cloves, cinnamon, pepper, mustard and celery seeds, and salt. Bring the mixture to a boil and boil for 1 minute, over medium heat. Add the remaining ingredients and return the mixture to a boil. Reduce the heat and simmer, stirring occasionally, for 2 hours or until the relish thickens. Ladle it into warmed, sterilized jars, leave to cool, and then seal. The jars can be opened after 1 month.

MAKES ABOUT 8 CUPS

*BELOW: Red Tomato and Fruit Relish*

# TAMARILLO CHUTNEY

*Tamarillos can be eaten raw, though some find them an acquired taste. They also make wonderful chutney and jam, and can be stewed for dessert or added to salsa.*

INGREDIENTS

20 tamarillos

4 white or brown onions, peeled

1 pound (500 g) cooking apples, peeled and cored

1 cup (5 ounces/155 g) golden raisins (sultanas)

3 cups (750 mL) malt vinegar

1 teaspoon sea salt

½ teaspoon ground cloves

1 teaspoon mustard seeds

1 teaspoon ground ginger

1 teaspoon cayenne pepper

2 cloves garlic, chopped

4½ cups (1½ pounds/750 g) brown sugar

To make it easy to remove the skins of the tamarillos, plunge them into a saucepan of boiling water and then immediately into cold water. Peel and chop the tamarillos, onions, and apples. Place all the ingredients in a large, nonreactive saucepan over medium heat. Bring the mixture to a boil and then simmer for 1½ to 2 hours, stirring occasionally, until the chutney thickens. Ladle the chutney into warmed, sterilized jars. Allow it to cool and then seal the jars. Store the chutney in a cool, dark place for up to 12 months. This chutney can be eaten after 4 weeks.

MAKES ABOUT 6 TO 8 CUPS

---

TAMARILLOS

The tamarillo is a tree tomato from Peru. It belongs to the *Solanaceae* family, as does the tomato. It has reddish-yellow to purple skin and is egg-shaped. Like a tomato, the flesh encloses edible seeds. Tamarillos have an acidic, slightly sweet taste, with an underlying tomato flavor. The fruit grows on a short-lived tree, propagated by seed or cutting, and makes an attractive addition to a home garden orchard in temperate to tropical climates.

---

*RIGHT: The elegant egg-shaped tamarillo makes a colorful and amusing still-life.*

# Herbs AND Spices

*Anything green that grew out of the mould*

*Was an excellent herb to our fathers of old.*

RUDYARD KIPLING

LEFT: *The equipment and foods you need to make herb-flavored wine vinegars.*

137

# HERB-FLAVORED WINE VINEGARS

*When you give this vinegar as a gift, strain the flavored vinegar into an attractive bottle and add a fresh herb sprig.*

INGREDIENTS

*6 sprigs of herb of choice, such as basil, rosemary, tarragon, dill, or thyme*

*3 cups (750 mL) good quality white wine or Champagne vinegar*

*6 black peppercorns*

Lightly bruise the herbs and put them into a wide-necked, sterilized bottle. Heat the wine or vinegar in a saucepan, add the peppercorns, and bring the liquid to boiling point. Remove the pan from the heat, cool the liquid to tepid, and pour it over the herbs. Seal and leave the wine vinegar in a sunny place to infuse for 2 weeks, shaking the bottle daily.

MAKES ABOUT 3 CUPS

# HERB-FLAVORED VIRGIN OLIVE OIL

*Use any herbs you like. Basil is very good, as is tarragon, and a mixture of thyme and sage has an excellent flavor. This method can be an ongoing process — just keep adding fresh sprigs to the oil bottle. Use the oil in dressings, for basting and marinating meats, and also in pasta dishes.*

INGREDIENTS

*8 sprigs of fresh basil or herb of choice*

*6 black peppercorns*

*3 cloves garlic, peeled and lightly bruised*

*3 cups (750 mL) good quality virgin olive oil*

Use a wide-necked bottle and fill it with the herbs. Add the peppercorns and garlic. Top up with the olive oil and seal well. Leave the oil in a sunny place to infuse for 4 weeks before using.

MAKES ABOUT 3 CUPS

# HERB-FLAVORED
# SEA SALT

*A little of this salt goes a long way and is far more interesting than plain salt, especially when barbecuing and grilling.*

INGREDIENTS
*¼ cup dried parsley flakes*
*2 tablespoons dried basil leaves*
*1 tablespoon dried marjoram or oregano leaves*
*1 teaspoon paprika*
*½ teaspoon dried thyme leaves*
*1 cup (8 ounces/250 g) sea salt*

Place all the ingredients in a blender or food processor and blend just enough to combine them. Store the flavored salt in an airtight jar on the kitchen counter with your other essential condiments.

MAKES ABOUT 1 CUP

*ABOVE: Fresh dill and sage — good basic flavorings for a caring cook.*

> SALTS
>
> Sea salt is the best salt for the table and cooking. It is naturally made from the effects of the sun and the wind. The large crystals can be ground in a salt mill or the flaky kind can be sprinkled directly onto food. Rock salt is hard and coarse but it can be among the finest of salts and should not be confused with non-edible freezing salt which is used for making ice creams. Common table salt is iodized and not comparable to crystal and rock salt.

# FLAVORED SUGARS

*Subtly flavored sugars can be used in everything from tea to cakes.*

RIGHT: *Flavored sugars are really handy to have on hand, especially when fresh herbs, spices, and fruit aren't available. The photograph shows citrus and scented geranium sugars, as well as ingredients for rose petal, spice, and vanilla sugars.*

FREEZING HERBS
*Most herbs can be frozen very successfully and the flavor preserves well. Store them in sealed plastic bags that have been flattened to expel the air. Alternatively, chop the leaves finely in a blender or food processor with a little water and freeze in ice-cube trays. When frozen, pack the ice cubes into freezer bags. The best herbs to freeze are parsley, chervil, chives, tarragon, dill, cilantro (coriander), basil, and mint.*

Select the flavoring you prefer and place the ingredient in a wide-necked, sterilized jar, pouring over enough white granulated sugar or superfine (caster) sugar to cover the item until your jar is filled. The quantity will vary according to the ingredient. A couple of geranium leaves should suffice but you will need many rose petals to fill even a small jar. You will also need to purchase several muslin bags if using spices.

*Rose petals.* Choose unblemished, dry petals with a deep perfume.

*Vanilla.* Use fresh, strong-scented vanilla pods which you may need to cut to fit into the selected jar. Use the vanilla sugar in cakes and desserts, topping up the sugar as it is used.

*Lavender.* Use fresh spikes cut from the stem. Eat lavender sugar within 2 months when the flavor is strongest.

*Scented geranium.* These leaves are grown in a variety of perfumes — cinnamon, rose, and lemon-scented — and all are ideal to flavor sugar. Geranium-scented sugar is especially good to flavor cakes.

*Lemon-scented verbena.* Place a few leaves in a jar, then add sugar, then add more leaves, and so on until the jar is filled. Use this sugar to flavor herbal teas.

*Citrus.* Remove strips of peel from 2 oranges or lemons. Place the peel in a jar of sugar and leave to infuse for a few days. Sprinkle over fresh fruit such as strawberries or dust the top of plain or citrus cakes.

*Spices.* Tie a mixture of spices into a muslin bag and then cover with sugar. An excellent combination is a few cloves, allspice berries, a cinnamon stick, a whole nutmeg, and a tiny piece of star anise as it is stronger than the other spices. Spiced sugar gives tea a lovely flavor.

# VANILLA BRANDY

*I keep this brandy in my pantry to pour over Christmas cakes and hot puddings. A drop or two is also delicious in espresso coffee sipped while you eat a rich chocolate after dinner!*

INGREDIENTS
*2 fresh vanilla beans*
*3 cups (750 mL) brandy*

Place the vanilla beans in a bottle of brandy. The finer the brandy, the better the flavor. Seal the bottle, label it, and allow it to infuse for at least 6 weeks. As the vanilla-flavored brandy is used up, keep topping it up with more brandy.
MAKES ABOUT 3 CUPS

# CANDIED ANGELICA

*Angelica is a good plant for an herb garden. Its attractive leaves make a pretty garnish and the candied stems can be used to decorate cakes.*

INGREDIENTS
*4 young, tender, fresh angelica*
  *stems*
*White granulated sugar*
*Superfine (caster) sugar*

*RIGHT: I store Vanilla Brandy in these antique Chinese flasks that I was lucky enough to inherit. Always use vanilla beans to add natural vanilla flavor.*

Cut the angelica stems into equal lengths, place them in a saucepan, cover with cold water, bring the water to a boil, and boil until just tender, about 5 minutes. Test if cooked with a fine skewer. Remove the stems from the water with a slotted spoon. Peel away the thin outer skin, which is a bit like celery. Place the stems back in the water, return it to a boil, and simmer until they turn a light green, about 5 minutes. Drain and dry the angelica pieces on a cake rack. Weigh the stems, then place them in a rectangular dish, making sure that the stems are not bent, and cover them with an equal weight of sugar. Cover the dish with a dishcloth and leave for 2 days. Empty the contents of the bowl into a saucepan, bring to a boil, and boil until the angelica is green again, about 5 to 10 minutes, then drain, roll the stems in superfine sugar, and dry on a cake rack. Store the candied angelica in an airtight jar in a cool, dry place. The candied angelica will keep indefinitely.

# PRESERVED GINGER

*Try to buy very young, pink-tipped ginger root for this preserve as it is less fibrous and more tender than older ginger, which is a darker yellow and tough-skinned.*

INGREDIENTS

1 pound (500 g) fresh young
  ginger
2 cups (1 pound/500 g) white
  granulated sugar
½ cup (125 mL) water

*LEFT: Stem ginger is preserved in syrup to make Preserved Ginger and packed into Chinese porcelain jars. It is delicious eaten with desserts or as a confection. Ginger is used in all the Asian countries, especially China.*

Scrape the ginger carefully with a small paring knife to remove the outside tissue. Cut the ginger into small pieces, about ⅜ inch (1 cm), and drop them into a bowl of cold water as you cut them. Leave aside for 1 hour, then drain. Place the ginger in a saucepan and just cover with cold water. Bring the water to a boil, cook the ginger for 5 minutes, and drain. Repeat the process, but this time bring the water to a boil, reduce the heat, and simmer for 30 minutes. The ginger should be just tender. Check with a fine skewer and drain. Place the sugar and the water in a small saucepan and stir well over medium heat until the sugar dissolves, about 10 minutes. Add the ginger and simmer for 20 minutes, stirring occasionally. Distribute the ginger between sterilized jars, add the syrup, and seal. Store the ginger in a cool, dark place for up to 12 months.
MAKES ABOUT 1 4-CUP JAR

# GINGER BEER

*Tangy homemade ginger beer is far superior to any commercial variety.*

INGREDIENTS

1½-inch (6 cm) piece fresh
  ginger, peeled
3 large lemons, sliced
1 teaspoon cream of tartar
2 cups (1 pound /500 g) white
  granulated sugar
20 cups (5 quarts/5 liters)
  boiling water
5 teaspoons fresh yeast

Flatten the ginger with the flat of a large knife to expel the juice. Place the ginger, lemon slices, cream of tartar, and sugar in a large bowl and pour over the boiling water. Stir well to dissolve the sugar. When tepid, stir in the yeast. Leave covered at room temperature for 24 to 30 hours.

Skim the frothy yeast off the top. Strain and pour the ginger beer into sterilized bottles with clip-top lids. Leave for 5 days before opening. Store the ginger beer in a cool, dark place.
MAKES ABOUT 6 QUARTS (6 LITERS)

# GRAINY MUSTARD

*For a different flavor, add 3 tablespoons of red or green peppercorns in brine.*

INGREDIENTS

*8 ounces (250 g) white mustard
  seeds*
*1¼ cups (310 mL) white wine
  vinegar, plus extra if
  necessary*
*2 tablespoons unflavored honey*
*1 tablespoon sea salt*

Grind the mustard seeds in a coffee grinder or a food mill to your preferred texture. Place the ground seeds in a bowl, stir in half the vinegar, and leave for 15 minutes. Stir in the remaining vinegar, honey, and salt. If the mixture is too dry, add more vinegar. Cover the bowl with a dishcloth and leave overnight. Check the consistency of the mustard and if it is too dry, add more liquid. Spoon the mustard into sterilized jars and seal. The mustard will keep in a cool, dark place for up to 12 months. It is ready to use after 1 month.

MAKES ABOUT 2 CUPS

# MINT JELLY

*This classic accompaniment to roast lamb can also be used to enliven other dishes.*

INGREDIENTS

*5 pounds (2.5 kg) cooking
  apples, roughly chopped*
*4 cups (1 liter) water*
*4 sprigs of mint*
*4 cups (1 liter) white wine
  vinegar*
*White granulated sugar*
*½ cup chopped, fresh mint
  leaves*

RIGHT: *Homemade Grainy
Mustard is far superior to
purchased mustard.*

Place the chopped apples in a large, nonreactive saucepan and add the water and mint sprigs. Bring the water to a boil over medium heat, reduce the heat to a simmer, and cook the apples until they are soft and pulpy, about 45 minutes. Add the vinegar, stir, and boil for 5 minutes. Ladle the mixture into a jelly bag and leave it to drip into a bowl without squeezing it for 12 hours or overnight. Discard the fruit pulp left in the bag. Measure the liquid in the bowl into the cleaned saucepan and for every 2½ cups (625 mL) liquid add 2 cups (500 g/1 lb) sugar. Stir the mixture over medium heat until the sugar dissolves and then increase the heat to boil rapidly for 10 to 15 minutes or until setting point is reached. Skim the surface of any scum. Stir in the chopped mint and leave the jelly to cool. Stir again, ladle the jelly into sterilized jars, and seal. The mint jelly can be used immediately or it will keep for 3 months.

MAKES ABOUT 6 CUPS

# SAGE JELLY

*Serve this jelly with roast chicken or pork.*

INGREDIENTS

*2 pounds (1 kg) cooking apples,
roughly chopped*

*1 cup loosely packed fresh sage
leaves*

*3 cups (750 mL) water*

*½ cup (125 mL) white wine
vinegar*

*White granulated sugar*

*Extra ½ cup sage leaves, as
small as possible*

Place the apples in a large, nonreactive pan and add the sage leaves, water, and vinegar. Cover the pan, bring the mixture to a boil, and cook until the apples are soft, about 10 minutes. Ladle the fruit and juice into a jelly bag and leave it to drip into a bowl overnight. Discard the fruit pulp left in the bag.

The next day, measure the juice into a jam pan or a large, wide saucepan and for every cup (250 mL) juice add 1 cup (8 ounces/250 g) sugar. Place the pan over medium heat and stir until the sugar dissolves. Bring the mixture to a rapid boil and cook until setting point is reached, about 30 to 40 minutes. Stir the small sage leaves into the jelly and cook for a further 2 minutes. Remove the pan from the heat, leave for 10 minutes, then stir. Ladle the jelly into warmed, sterilized jars, and seal.

MAKES ABOUT 1 CUP

# CHILE SAUCE

*Pungent chile sauce is at home with nearly any dish, from fish and meat to vegetables.*

INGREDIENTS

*½ cup (2 ounces/60 g) chile
(chilli) powder*

*3 cups (1 pound/500 g) sugar*

*3 cups (750 mL) white vinegar*

*2 cups (10 ounces/310 g)
golden raisins (sultanas)*

*2 cloves garlic, chopped*

*1½ teaspoons ground ginger*

*2 teaspoons mustard seeds*

*3 teaspoons sea salt*

Place all the ingredients in a large, nonreactive pan. Bring the mixture to a boil over medium heat, stirring constantly for 15 minutes. Remove the saucepan from the heat and allow the mixture to cool, then pour it into a blender or a food processor and blend to a sauce consistency. Pour the sauce into sterilized bottles. Store in a cool, dark place for up to 12 months. It is ready to use as soon as required.

MAKES ABOUT 4 CUPS

# PRESERVED WHOLE CHILES

*Use red or green chiles or a mixture of both. This is an excellent way to ensure you always have chiles on hand.*

INGREDIENTS
4 ounces (125 g) fresh chiles
    (chillies)
½ cup (4 ounces/125 g) white
    granulated sugar
1½ cups (375 mL) white wine
    vinegar
6 black peppercorns

If possible, leave a small stem on the chiles to prevent the open stem end from becoming soft. Pack the chiles into a wide-necked jar. Place the sugar, vinegar, and peppercorns in a saucepan over medium heat and bring the mixture to a boil. As soon as it has boiled, pour the hot vinegar over the chiles, almost to the top of the jar, and seal well. The chiles will keep for 12 months stored in the refrigerator.

MAKES ABOUT ½ CUP

# HARISSA

*Keeping a layer of oil on top of the Harissa ensures that it doesn't dry out.*

INGREDIENTS
8 ounces (250 g) dried hot red
    chiles (chillies)
3 cloves garlic, chopped
1 teaspoon mustard seeds
½ teaspoon sea salt
½ cup (125 mL) extra virgin
    olive oil, plus 2 tablespoons
    extra

Place the chiles in a bowl and cover them with hot water. Leave them to soak for 2 hours. Drain and pat them dry with paper towels. Transfer the chiles to a food processor or a blender, add the garlic, mustard seeds, and salt, and blend slowly, adding the olive oil in a slow stream, to make a thin, smooth paste. Spoon the harissa into a sterilized jar and pour the extra olive oil on top. Seal and store in the refrigerator for up to 12 months.

MAKES ABOUT 1 CUP

---

HOT CHILE!
To test the pungency of a chile, touch the chile with the tip of your tongue and wait. If after a minute it causes a burning sensation it is a very hot one. If you feel nothing, eat a little. Now judge whether it is medium or mild.

---

# More Pantry Pleasures

The best olive is gold, the second silver,

the third is worth nothing.

TUSCAN SAYING

LEFT: *Freshly brined olives, the first step in the process to making them edible.*

# LEMON AND HERB OLIVES

*Kalamata are the best black olives, so use them if they are available.*

INGREDIENTS
*1 pound (500 g) green olives*
*2 lemons, sliced*
*1 teaspoon coriander seeds*
*2 sprigs of rosemary*
*2 sprigs of thyme*
*2 cloves garlic, peeled*
*1 tablespoon black peppercorns*
*Bay leaves*
*1 pound (500 g) black olives*
*Extra virgin olive oil*

Use a wide-necked jar to facilitate filling and serving. Drain and rinse the green olives if they are in brine. Place a layer of green olives in the bottom of a sterilized jar, top with a layer of sliced lemon, then a sprinkling of herbs and sliced garlic, followed by a layer of black olives. Continue the layers until the jar is filled. Add the olive oil, seal, and store the olives in a cool place.

MAKES ABOUT 1 6-CUP JAR

# OLIVE RELISH

*This relish makes a wonderful dip or a spread for crostini, toast, or fresh crusty bread. Without the tomato paste it is known as tapénade.*

INGREDIENTS
*3 ounces (90 g) anchovy fillets*
*1½ cups (7 ounces /225 g) black olives, pitted and chopped*
*2 tablespoons capers, chopped*
*2 cloves garlic, chopped*
*2 tablespoons fresh lemon juice*
*Freshly ground black pepper*
*2 tablespoons sun-dried tomato paste*

Place all the ingredients, except the sun-dried tomato paste, in a mortar and pestle, food processor or blender and blend to the desired consistency of paste, rough or smooth. Stir in the sun-dried tomato paste. Spoon into a sterilized jar. Store the relish in the refrigerator.

MAKES ABOUT 1½ CUPS

*RIGHT: Fresh olives, soon to be marinated into Lemon and Herb Olives or made into an Olive Relish.*

# SPICY NUTS

*Prepare these nuts to serve with drinks. Just pop them in the oven for 10 minutes to warm or refresh them.*

INGREDIENTS
1 cup (5 ounces/155 g)
  unsalted peanuts
1 cup (5 ounces/155 g)
  unsalted cashew nuts
1 cup (5 ounces/155 g)
  blanched almonds
⅔ cup (3 ounces/90 g) hazelnuts
1½ tablespoons butter, melted
2 teaspoons Worcestershire
  sauce
4 drops Tabasco sauce
1 teaspoon soy sauce
2 tablespoons sea salt

Combine all the nuts in a bowl. In another bowl, mix together the butter and sauces and then pour the mixture over the nuts, stirring with a wooden spoon. Spread the nuts onto a baking tray lined with baking paper and sprinkle with the salt. Place the tray in a preheated oven at 315°F (160 °C) and cook for 20 to 25 minutes, shaking the tray several times. Remove the nuts from the oven, cool completely, and then store them in an airtight jar for up to 3 months.
MAKES ABOUT 4 CUPS

NUTS ARE GOOD FOR YOU
No cook should be without nuts or nut oil; not only are nuts rich in protein and oils, but they contain vitamins, calcium, and iron in their oils and also antioxidants which may help in the prevention of cancer.

# NUTS IN HONEY

*A healthy treat. For a not-so-healthy, but delicious-tasting treat, dip one end of each nutty piece into melted chocolate. Use unsalted peanuts in this recipe.*

INGREDIENTS
1 cup (11 ounces/340 g) honey
⅓ cup (90 g) butter
½ cup (3 ounces/90 g) whole
  almonds, blanched
½ cup (3 ounces/90 g) peanuts
1¼ cup (3 ounces/90 g) toasted
  shredded coconut
⅓ cup (2 ounces/60 g) toasted
  sesame seeds

Place the honey and butter in a medium-sized saucepan and stir over low heat until the butter has melted. Simmer gently for 5 minutes, until the mixture is golden. Remove the pan from the heat and stir in the nuts, coconut, and toasted sesame seeds. Drop spoonfuls of the mixture onto a tray lined with parchment paper. Allow to set, then store in an airtight container. They will keep for up to 3 months.
MAKES ABOUT 60

# MANGO CHUTNEY

*I like to serve this tasty relish with curries, cold meats, or cheese platters.*

INGREDIENTS
1½ cups (8 ounces/250 g)
   brown sugar
1½ cups (375 mL) white
   vinegar
1 large onion, chopped
2 cloves garlic, finely chopped
1 teaspoon ground cinnamon
½ teaspoon ground allspice
½ teaspoon ground cloves
¼ teaspoon cayenne pepper
1 teaspoon chopped ginger
½ cup (3 ounces/90 g) raisins
1 teaspoon mustard seeds
4 pounds (2 kg) ripe mangoes
Juice of 1 lemon

Place all the ingredients in a large saucepan, except for the mangoes and lemon juice. Bring the mixture to a boil and simmer for 45 minutes, stirring occasionally. Meanwhile, peel and slice the mangoes, place them in a bowl, and add the lemon juice. Add the mangoes to the hot vinegar mixture and simmer until the fruit is tender, about 30 minutes. Ladle the chutney into warmed, sterilized jars, allow to cool, and then seal. The chutney will be ready to eat after 3 weeks.
MAKES ABOUT 8 CUPS

# BANANA JAM

*The tropical flavors of this jam will make even toast seem exotic.*

INGREDIENTS
4 pounds (2 kg) ripe bananas
¾ cup (185 mL) canned
   pineapple juice
½ cup (125 mL) lemon juice
4 cups (2 pounds/1 kg) white
   granulated sugar
2 ounces (60 g) powdered citrus
   pectin
½ cup (3 ounces/90 g) raisins

Peel the bananas and roughly mash half of them and slice the other half. Place them in a jam pan or a large, wide saucepan and immediately add the pineapple and lemon juices. Stir in the sugar, pectin, and raisins. Mix well, then place the pan over high heat. Bring the mixture to a boil, stirring continuously, and cook at this heat for 5 minutes or until setting point is reached. Ladle the jam into warmed, sterilized jars and cool. Cover and seal the jars. Leave the jam for 2 weeks before using it.
MAKES ABOUT 4 CUPS

# MARINATED GOAT'S CHEESES

*Include these cheeses as part of an antipasto to spread on crusty bread or crostini, or keep them handy to spice up pasta dishes.*

### INGREDIENTS
*10 small, mature goat's milk cheeses (chèvre)*
*4 cloves garlic, peeled and sliced*
*10 black peppercorns*
*4 fresh, small, red chiles (chillies)*
*1 sprig of rosemary*
*2 sprigs of sage*
*2 sprigs of thyme*
*2 bay leaves*
*Extra virgin olive oil*

Carefully pack the goat's cheeses into a large, wide-necked, sterilized jar with a tight-fitting lid. As you layer the cheeses, decoratively arrange the garlic, peppercorns, chiles, and herbs in and around the cheeses. Pour over olive oil to reach the top of the jar. Dispel any air pockets by running a skewer down the inside of the jar. Store in the refrigerator for up to 3 months but bring the cheeses to room temperature before serving.

MAKES ABOUT 1 4-CUP JAR

*RIGHT: The recipe for these delectable Marinated Goat's Cheeses can also be used to marinate cubes of feta cheese.*

# FEIJOA JAM

*As with many fruits, the season for feijoas is short and we often have too many at once. Jam is a good way of storing them to eat at a later date.*

### INGREDIENTS
*2 pounds (1 kg) feijoas, peeled and sliced*
*½ cup (125 mL) water*
*Juice and zest of 1 lemon*
*4 cups (2 pounds/1 kg) white granulated sugar, warmed*

Place the feijoas in a jam pan or a large, wide saucepan, and add the water, lemon juice, and zest. Bring the mixture to a boil over medium heat and cook the fruit until it is soft, about 15 minutes. Add the warmed sugar and stir until it dissolves. Bring the jam to a rapid boil and boil without stirring until the mixture reaches setting point, about 20 minutes. Pour the jam into warmed, sterilized jars, cool, and then seal. The jam can be eaten immediately.

MAKES ABOUT 6 TO 8 CUPS

# INDEX